HANDBOOK OF

Mathematical and Statistical Techniques for Accountants

HANDBOOK OF

Mathematical and Statistical Techniques for Accountants

Donald H. Taylor, Ph. D., CPA

Prentice-Hall Inc.

Englewood Cliffs, N.J.

Prentice-Hall International, Inc., *London*
Prentice-Hall of Australia, Pty. Ltd., *Sydney*
Prentice-Hall of Canada, Ltd., *Toronto*
Prentice-Hall of India Private Ltd., *New Delhi*
Prentice-Hall of Japan, Inc., *Tokyo*
Prentice-Hall of Southeast Asia Pte. Ltd., *Singapore*
Whitehall Books, Ltd., *Wellington, New Zealand*

This publication is designed to provide accurate and authoritative information in regard to the subject matter covered. It is sold with the understanding that the publisher is not engaged in rendering legal, accounting, or other professional service. If legal advice or other expert assistance is required, the services of a competent professional person should be sought.

—From a Declaration of Principles jointly adopted
by a Committee of the American Bar Association
and a Committee of Publishers and Associations.

Library of Congress Cataloging in Publication Data

Taylor, Donald H
  Handbook of mathematical and statistical techniques for accountants.

  Includes index.
  1. Business mathematics. 2. Accounting.
3. Statistics. I. Title. II. Title: Mathematical and statistical techniques for accountants.
HF5691.T36   657   77-6694
ISBN 0-13-380345-7

Printed in the United States of America

Donald H. Taylor is an Associate Professor of Accounting at **About The Author**
the University of Arkansas. He received a B.S. in Accounting
from Louisiana Polytechnic Institute (now Louisiana Tech
University) and an M.B.A. and a Ph.D. from Louisiana State
University.

The author has had several years of public accounting experience and is a CPA in Texas, Louisiana, and Arkansas. He
has conducted programs for the National Association of Accountants and for the Arkansas Society of Certified Public
Accountants, and he has written numerous articles for
professional and technical journals.

He has conducted courses in computer logic and programming, as well as auditing, systems, and statistical applications
in accounting.

The author is a member of the American Institute of Certified
Public Accountants, the Arkansas Society of Certified Public
Accountants, the American Accounting Association, the
National Association of Accountants, the American Institute
for Decision Sciences, Beta Alpha Psi, Phi Kappa Phi, and
Omicron Delta Kappa.

Dr. Taylor is also the author of *Auditing: Integrated Concepts
and Procedures* (Wiley/Hamilton Publishing Company).

Accountants are in the forefront of data collection and information reporting, and as such should have access to as many quantitative tools as possible. This book is a reference guide for public, industrial, and governmental accountants, as well as operations people, who have a need to use statistical and quantitative techniques in their particular organizations. The reason for selecting the topics contained in this book is the relationship they have with current conventional accounting techniques studied in the classroom and successfully implemented in business and professional practice. In addition, the techniques described have a wide variety of applications in all phases of business and should benefit management in any working environment. Here are some examples:

A Word From the Author

1. In chapters 1 and 2, probability analysis is combined with capital budgeting methodology to provide answers as to the profitability of long-term capital asset investments and the least expensive way to finance such investments.
2. In chapter 3, certain statistical sampling concepts are tied together with standard cost variance analysis to derive answers on the feasibility of variance investigation. In chapter 8, other statistical sampling concepts are shown to be beneficial in helping auditors engage in a more efficient sampling process.
3. In chapters 4 and 5, regression, correlation and exponential smoothing analyses are used in conjunction with accountants' traditional planning and control techniques to produce more profitable ways of budgeting revenues and costs for future time periods.
4. In chapter 6, linear programming is combined with accountants' traditional methods of cost-profit-volume analyses to produce more efficient ways of allocating advertising and research dollars to company segments.

5. In chapters 7 and 9, simple quantitative techniques are related to traditional audit procedures to supply practicing accountants with better ways to use random number tables in their sampling process and more efficient ways to use internal control questionnaires.

The reason for addressing this book primarily to accountants is that they are skilled in the use of many other quantitative techniques learned in the classroom and later applied in practice (standard cost analysis, flexible budgeting, cost accumulation, control and reporting, segment analysis, capital budgeting, and many more). Also, accountants have established channels of communication with clients and management because of their experience in accumulating and reporting quantitative information. It is only natural, then, that accountants should be the group to use the book's statistical and quantitative concepts to help their companies and/or themselves to improve profits and operate more efficiently.

Here are some questions that will be answered by reading and studying this book:

1. How many years must a capital asset be used, what depreciation rate and method must be chosen and what end-of-life salvage value must be obtainable to justify the acquisition of that capital asset?
2. What is the expected net present value of acquiring a capital asset if probabilities are attached to several possible expected lives?
3. Is it less expensive to buy or lease a capital asset? What effect does the probability of different asset lives have on the buy/lease decision?
4. How large should the variances from standard costs be to justify the expenses of investigation? What rules should be employed to decide when variances from standard cost should be investigated?
5. How should costs that have a fixed and variable element be budgeted for future periods?
6. How can a company ascertain whether there is sufficient

correlation between a certain type of activity and a certain cost?

7. How can historical data be used to separate the fixed and variable portions of a cost?
8. How can future sales be forecasted using simple linear and nonlinear techniques?
9. How can advertising or research dollars be allocated among product lines, divisions or territories to maximize company profits?
10. How much production time should be devoted to each product line to maximize profits?
11. How can attribute and variable sampling techniques be combined to produce more reliable and efficient sampling results?
12. How can more efficient use be made of random number tables in the audit of unnumbered documents?
13. How can auditors tie in internal control questionnaires with statistical sampling objectives?

An additional and special highlight of the book is the computer programs in the last chapter. The FORTRAN programs are applications of many of the statistical and quantitative techniques illustrated throughout the book. The programs, with minor modifications, can be run on any compatible computer equipment.

A distinct advantage of using these computer programs is the ability to obtain a wide variety of hypothetical answers with different inputs. For example, in the chapter 1 capital budgeting application different estimated asset lives, depreciation rates, tax rates and salvage values can be used as inputs in the program. The variety of results obtained from these different inputs allows the user to make more efficient and profitable decisions.

The illustrations and explanations in the book are numbered in step-by-step fashion and are easy to follow. These numbers are placed on end-of-chapter flowcharts of the same applications. They are also keyed alongside explanations accompanying the computer program listings in the last chapter.

It is hoped and anticipated that use of the techniques illustrated in this book will result in a more profitable and efficient operation for the accountant's client and management personnel.

Donald H. Taylor, Ph.D., CPA

Contents

3   THE USE OF PROBABILITY IN SETTING
    CONTROL LIMITS FOR VARIANCES FROM
    STANDARDS

4   THE USE OF THE LEAST SQUARES TECHNIQUE
    TO DETERMINE THE PATTERN OF REVENUES
    AND COSTS

5   THE USE OF EXPONENTIAL SMOOTHING
    TO FORECAST REVENUES AND COSTS

6   THE USE OF LINEAR PROGRAMMING IN THE
    DEPLOYMENT OF RESOURCES TO DIFFERENT
    SEGMENT LINES

1

The Use of Probability in the Depreciable Asset Investment Decision

The present value approach to evaluating long-term investments is an established procedure in many companies. In addition, some firms are incorporating probability analysis into their long-term investment decision.

An example is a model built by Northern Natural Gas, Omaha, Nebraska.* Probabilities were assigned to various input factors that go into the investment decision. Several rates of return were generated, coupled with the probability of each rate occurring.

This type of simulation is valuable because the company can see what would happen if the investment were made a number of times. All of these simulated results can be converted into an estimate of what to expect when the investment is actually made.

This chapter contains similar techniques which will help accountants make a positive contribution to the investment decision. Each option can have a range of values generated, and comparisons can be made among the various results.

Many of the inputs in this model are taken from the data base generated by accountants. Therefore, they are in a unique position to render valuable aid to their company by suggesting a capital budgeting model of this type. Consulting accountants can perform the same service for their clients.

*Geiler, Louis E., "Analysis of Uncertainty in Capital Expenditures," *Management Accounting,* January, 1970, pp. 32-36.

The Traditional Analytical Techniques Used in the Long-Range Investment Decision

The simplest (and probably most popular) analysis is a model that demonstrates how long it will take for the company to "get their money back." An example of this model is shown in Illustration 1. Assume that the cost of the contemplated investment is $10,000 and that the expected yearly returns or "cash flows" are $3,000.

ILLUSTRATION 1
THE PAYBACK METHOD OF EVALUATING
DEPRECIABLE ASSET INVESTMENT DECISIONS

Investment Cost	$10,000
Divided by Anticipated Cash Flows per Year	3,000
Payback Period	3.3 Years

Although the above analysis is useful, it falls short in many respects. No recognition is given either to the total economic life of the asset or to the time value of money.

The present-value technique is a more sophisticated approach. It considers the cash flows over the estimated useful life of the investment. This present value is then measured against the cost to help determine the feasibility of the project. Illustration 2 shows this type of analysis. A figure in parentheses is an outlay; a figure without parentheses is a benefit. The assumptions are listed below and are keyed to the example by letter.

(a) The investment cost is $10,000. In this model, the reader can assume that the outlay is a planned purchase from an outsider.

(b) The economic life (not necessarily the physical life) of the asset to the company is assumed to be five years.

(c) The estimated salvage value at the end of five years is $1,000. Previous company experience would serve as a guide here.

(d) The salvage value for tax purposes is assumed to be the same as the salvage value for book purposes. The reader can refer to Internal Revenue guidelines for an appropriate range of figures for different types of assets.

ILLUSTRATION 2
THE EXCESS-PRESENT-VALUE METHOD
OF EVALUATING DEPRECIABLE ASSET INVESTMENT DECISIONS
FIVE-YEAR LIFE

	(1) End of Year	(2) Cash Flow Before Tax	(3) Tax On Cash Flow*	(4) Cash Flow After Tax (2) – (3)	(5) Present-Value Factor @ 10%[f]	(6) Present Value (4) x (5)
Cost	0	$ –	$ –	$ –	–	$(10,000)[a]
Flow	1	3,000[h]	600	2,400	.909	2,182
Flow	2	3,000	600	2,400	.826	1,982
Flow	3	3,000	600	2,400	.751	1,802
Flow	4	3,000	600	2,400	.683	1,639
Flow	5	3,000	600	2,400	.621	1,490
Salvage Value	5[b]	–	–	1,000[c]	.621	621
						$ (284)[i]

*$10,000	Cost
(1,000)	Estimated Salvage Value[d]
$ 9,000	Depreciable Amount
X 20%	
$ 1,800	Year Depreciation[e]
X 50%	Tax Rate[g]
$ 900	Depreciation Shield
$ 3,000	Cash Flow Before Tax
X 50%	Tax Rate
$ 1,500	Tax on Flow Without Depreciation Shield
(900)	Shield
$ 600	Tax on Flow

(e) Depreciation is straight line. Within certain restrictions, the company may choose the method desired.

(f) The discount rate is 10 percent. It can generally be thought of as the minimum acceptable rate of return, after taxes, that the company will accept on investments of this type. The present-value factors are the present values of $1 to be received year 1, year 2, etc. (the present value of an amount, not the present value of an annuity).

(g) The assumed tax rate for the entire economic life is 50 percent.

(h) The incremental cash flow, before taxes, is $3,000 a year as the result of acquiring the asset. Cash flow refers to

21

net income before the deduction for depreciation (the major noncash determinant of net income).

(i) The bracketed $284 represents the amount by which the cost exceeds the estimated present value of the benefits. If the final figure is bracketed, the company should have other reasons for making the investment. If the final figure is not bracketed (benefits exceed cost), the company will have *one* reason to make the investment.

Evaluation of the Traditional Methods

The excess-present-value method as presented in Illustration 2 is an example of a deterministic model. Although different assumptions can be made about each type of input, the user will arrive at only one estimated total. Assume, for instance, that a four-year life and a $2,000 salvage value were placed into the model. The results are shown in Illustration 3.

ILLUSTRATION 3
THE EXCESS-PRESENT-VALUE METHOD OF
EVALUATING DEPRECIABLE ASSET INVESTMENT DECISIONS
FOUR-YEAR LIFE

	(1) End of Year	(2) Cash Flow Before Tax	(3) Tax On Cash Flow*	(4) Cash Flow After Tax (2) − (3)	(5) Present-Value Factor @ 10%	(6) Present Value (4) x (5)
Cost	0	$ −	$ −	$ −	−	$(10,000)
Flow	1	3,000	500	2,500	.909	2,273
Flow	2	3,000	500	2,500	.826	2,065
Flow	3	3,000	500	2,500	.751	1,878
Flow	4	3,000	500	2,500	.683	1,708
Salvage Value	4	−	−	2,000	.683	1,366
						$ (710)

*$10,000	Cost	$ 3,000		Cash Flow Before Tax
(2,000)	Estimated Salvage Value	× 50%		Tax Rate
$ 8,000	Depreciable Amount	$ 1,500		Tax on Flow Without Depreciation Shield
× 25%	Depreciation Rate	(1,000)		Shield
$ 2,000	Yearly Depreciation	$ 500		Tax on Flow
× 50%	Tax Rate			
$ 1,000	Depreciation Shield			

The deterministic model, therefore, is useful if management is sure of its inputs. For example, if five years is the only economic life that is considered probable and if $1,000 is the only contemplated salvage value, the excess-present-value at the bottom of Illustration 2 is appropriate. Likewise, if four years is the only reasonable estimate of economic life and if a $2,000 salvage value is the only estimate, then the Illustration 3 total is appropriate.

Introduction of Probability into the Model

It is unlikely that a company will have the degree of certainty implied in Illustrations 2 and 3. It is more reasonable to assume that each input factor has a *range* of values and that each possible value has a subjective probability associated with it. To elaborate on this point, one of the inputs to the excess-present-value model should be re-examined.

The economic life. In the deterministic model, five and four years, respectively, are used, but no probability is associated with either of these economic lives. Prior experience may indicate that the company has made decisions in the past to use similar fixed assets from four to five years. The records may also show that approximately 30 percent of the time four years was chosen and that approximately 70 percent of the time five years was selected. If no better evidence is available, this range of economic lives should be built into the model, along with the related probabilities.

Illustration 4 is an example of the numerical results if the totals of Illustrations 2 and 3 are multiplied by the probabilities assumed in the previous paragraph.

If the deterministic model in Illustration 2 is used by itself, the reader is left with the impression that the investment, if made, will lose $284 (a loss in the sense that the desired rate of return is not earned). The probabilistic model, shown above, indicates that the expected loss is $412. In addition, some valuable information about the possible range of losses is also revealed. There is a reasonable chance that $710 will be lost. While a $284 loss may be tolerable, a 30 percent chance of a $710 loss may persuade the company to ignore the investment.

ILLUSTRATION 4
THE APPLICATION OF PROBABILITY
TO THE TOTALS CALCULATED IN
ILLUSTRATIONS 2 AND 3

No. of Years of Estimated Life	Excess-Present-Value Totals from Illustrations 2 and 3	Probability That Asset Will Be Used This Many Years	Expected Excess Present Value
4	$(710)	.30	$(213)
5	(284)	.70	(199)
			$(412)

The Additional Versatility of the Probabilistic Model

The models explained in Illustrations 2 and 3 are flexible in the sense that all other input factors can be held constant while one or more inputs are allowed to vary. This provides *one* present value total for every combination of inputs. It provides some assistance to the company seeking quantitative investment guidelines. Its disadvantage, however, is that it still has too much rigidity. There is an implication of certainty that tends to contradict the company's usual feelings about long-range projects.

The model summarized in Illustration 4 and detailed in later illustrations is more versatile. The user may attach probabilities to each estimated life and a *range* of present-value totals will be generated. The reader may change other inputs and receive an entirely different set of figures. For example, if probabilities are placed on three estimates of useful life with a 50 percent tax rate, three present-value totals will be produced. Using the same three estimates and the same probabilities, the 50 percent tax rate can be changed to 45 percent and three additional sets of figures are obtained.

Accountants can use their knowledge of the system to advise management on the amount of each input. Judgment is required to select the range of economic lives and the probability associated with each estimate. For some factors, such as cost and tax rate, objectively determined figures should be available.

In the remainder of the chapter a set of calculations are developed that use a range of estimated lives from five to seven years. A step-by-step approach is explained, followed by the output (Illustration 5). A flowchart is drawn with the appropriate steps keyed to the symbols (Illustration 6).

Illustration of the Probabilistic Model

Step 1. Determine:
  (A) The investment cost—example in top figure in column (6), Illustration 5.
  (B) The number of estimates of economic life—three.
  (C) The probability of each estimate—example in column (8), Illustration 5.

Step 2. Estimate the actual salvage values—example in bottom figure in column (4), Illustration 5.

Step 3. Introduce the tax rate—50%.

Step 4. Introduce the present-value percentage—example in column (5), Illustration 5.

Step 5. Estimate the cash flow before tax—example in column (2), Illustration 5.

Step 6. Calculate the tax on the cash flow before tax—examples of results at bottom of Illustration 5.

Step 7. Subtract the result of step 6 from the result of step 5 to derive cash flow after tax—example of result in column (4) of Illustration 5.

Step 8. Multiply the result of step 7 times the present-value factor—example of result in column (6) of Illustration 5.

Step 9. Repeat steps 5-8 for each appropriate year.

Step 10. Multiply the result of step 2 times the present-value factor—example of result in bottom figure in column (6), Illustration 5.

Step 11. Subtract all nonbracketed figures in column (6), Illustration 5—example of result in column (7), Illustration 5.

Step 12. Multiply the result of step 11 times the probability percentage—example of result in column (9), Illustration 5.

Step 13. Repeat steps 2-12 for each different estimate of economic life.

Step 14. Determine the grand total of all the expected excess-value amounts—example of result at bottom of column (9), Illustration 5.

ILLUSTRATION 5
EXAMPLE OF OUTPUT GENERATED BY
THE PROBABILITY MODEL

(1) End of Year	(2) Cash Flow Before Tax	(3) Tax on Cash Flow*	(4) Cash Flow After Tax (2) − (3)	(5) Present-Value Factor @ 10%	(6) Present Value (4) x (5)	(7) Excess Present Value	(8) Proba-bility	(9) Expected Excess Present Value (7) x (8)
			FIVE-YEAR LIFE					
Cost 0	$ −	$ −	$ −	−	$(10,000)			
Flow 1	2,600	500	2,100	.909	1,909			
Flow 2	2,600	500	2,100	.826	1,735			
Flow 3	2,600	500	2,100	.751	1,577			
Flow 4	2,600	500	2,100	.683	1,434			
Flow 5	2,600	500	2,100	.621	1,304			
Salvage Value 5	−	−	2,000	.621	1,242	$(799)	.20	$(160)
			SIX-YEAR LIFE					
Cost 0	−	−	−	−	$(10,000)			
Flow 1	2,600	550	2,050	.909	1,863			
Flow 2	2,600	550	2,050	.826	1,693			
Flow 3	2,600	550	2,050	.751	1,540			
Flow 4	2,600	550	2,050	.683	1,400			
Flow 5	2,600	550	2,050	.621	1,273			
Flow 6	2,600	550	2,050	.564	1,156			
Salvage Value 6	−	−	1,000	.564	564	$(511)	.20	$(102)

SEVEN-YEAR LIFE

Cost	0	—	—	—	—	$(10,000)
Flow	1	2,600	650	1,950	.909	1,773
Flow	2	2,600	650	1,950	.826	1,611
Flow	3	2,600	650	1,950	.751	1,464
Flow	4	2,600	650	1,950	.683	1,332
Flow	5	2,600	650	1,950	.621	1,211
Flow	6	2,600	650	1,950	.564	1,100
Flow	7	2,600	650	1,950	.513	1,000
Salvage Value	7	—	—	900	.513	462
				$ (47)	.60	$ (28)
						$(290)

*CALCULATION OF TAX

	Five-Year Life	Six-Year Life	Seven-Year Life
Cost	$10,000	$10,000	$10,000
Salvage Value	2,000	1,000	900
Depreciable amount	$ 8,000	$ 9,000	$ 9,100
Depreciation rate	20%	16.6%	14.3%
Depreciation	$ 1,600	$ 1,500	$ 1,300
Tax rate	50%	50%	50%
Depreciation shield	$ 800	$ 750	$ 650
Cash flow before tax	$ 2,600	$ 2,600	$ 2,600
Tax before shield	1,300	1,300	1,300
Shield	(800)	(750)	(650)
Tax on Flow	$ 500	$ 550	$ 650

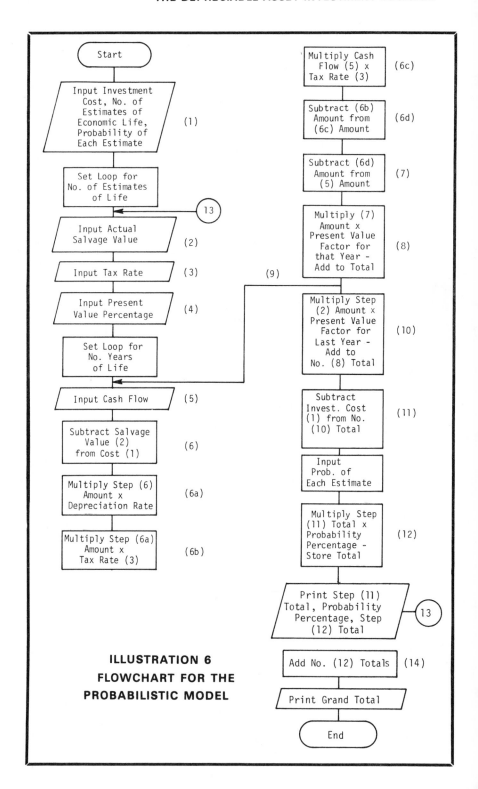

**ILLUSTRATION 6
FLOWCHART FOR THE
PROBABILISTIC MODEL**

The summary section of Illustration 5 is an example of the ranges of dollars and numbers that are obtained when *this* particular set of figures is used. Here are some of the advantages of this method.

Critique of Model Results

1. The estimated loss of $290 is a better evaluation of the feasibility of the project than either $(799), $(511) or $(47). If the deterministic model for the seven-year life is used as the sole guide, the investment might be made (unless intangible factors reversed the decision). The $(290) indicates, however, that the company needs to give the investment a second thought. It is quite possible that a bad decision could be avoided, thus saving the user a considerable amount of money.

2. There is a 40 percent chance that the company will earn a rate of return that is considerably less than the minimum 10 percent (this can loosely be referred to as losing money.) There is also a 20 percent chance that the loss will be about $800. The user of this model must decide whether it is worthwhile to accept this risk. A distribution of the type shown at the end of Illustration 5 provides management with the information to help make this decision.

3. The reader may change the inputs (as in Illustration 7) if he feels that other assumptions are more realistic. Each shift in a variable produces three different sets of figures (as in Illustration 8). Several sets can be obtained and comparisons made between the sets.

ILLUSTRATION 7
COMPARISON BETWEEN INPUTS FOR
ILLUSTRATIONS 5 AND 8

	Input Factors That Result in Illustration 5 Output	Input Factors That Result in Illustration 8 Output
Investment (Estimate)	$10,000	$10,000
Estimated Lives	5, 6, 7 Years	5, 6, 7 Years
Estimated Salvage Values	$2,000, $1,000, $900	$1,500, $1,000, $200
Tax Rate	50%	50%
Present-Value Rate	10%	8%
Cash Flows	$2,600 a Year	$3,000 a Year
Depreciation Method	Straight Line	Straight Line
Probability of Each Estimated Life	20%, 20%, 60%	30%, 30%, 40%

ILLUSTRATION 8
EXAMPLE OF OUTPUT GENERATED BY THE
PROBABILITY MODEL IF CERTAIN ASSUMPTIONS
ARE CHANGED

	End of Year	Cash Flow Before Tax	Tax on Cash Flow	Cash Flow After Tax	Present-Value Factor @ 8%	Present Value	Excess Present Value	Proba-bility	Expected Excess Present Value
FIVE-YEAR LIFE									
Cost	0	$ -	$ -	$ -	-	$(10,000)			
Flow	1	3,000	650	2,350	.926	2,176			
Flow	2	3,000	650	2,350	.857	2,014			
Flow	3	3,000	650	2,350	.794	1,866			
Flow	4	3,000	650	2,350	.735	1,727			
Flow	5	3,000	650	2,350	.681	1,600			
Salvage Value	5	-	-	1,500	.681	1,022	$ 405	.30	$ 122
SIX-YEAR LIFE									
Cost	0	-	-	-	-	$(10,000)			
Flow	1	3,000	750	2,250	.926	2,084			
Flow	2	3,000	750	2,250	.857	1,928			
Flow	3	3,000	750	2,250	.794	1,787			
Flow	4	3,000	750.	2,250	.735	1,654			
Flow	5	3,000	750	2,250	.681	1,532			
Flow	6	3,000	750	2,250	.630	1,418			
Salvage Value	6	-	-	1,000	.630	630	$1,033	.30	$ 310
SEVEN-YEAR LIFE									
Cost	0	-	-	-	-	$(10,000)			
Flow	1	3,000	800	2,200	.926	2,037			
Flow	2	3,000	800	2,200	.857	1,885			
Flow	3	3,000	800	2,200	.794	1,747			
Flow	4	3,000	800	2,200	.735	1,617			
Flow	5	3,000	800	2,200	.681	1,498			
Flow	6	3,000	800	2,200	.630	1,386			
Flow	7	3,000	800	2,200	.583	1,283			
Salvage Value	7	-	-	200	.583	117	$1,570	.40	$ 628
									$1,060

2

The Use of Probability
in the
Lease-Purchase Decision
for Depreciable Assets

Essentially, the capital budgeting *financing* decision is a choice of leasing or purchasing an asset. The following illustrations show the methodology that can be used to determine inherent cost savings of one financing arrangement over another.

The numerical model for depreciable items can have many forms, one of which is shown in Illustrations 1 and 2. A bracketed figure refers to a payment and a nonbracketed figure refers to a benefit.

The Deterministic Model

ILLUSTRATION 1
PURCHASE ALTERNATIVE FOR THE DETERMINISTIC MODEL — FIVE-YEAR LIFE

	(1) End of Year	(2) Amount	(3) Tax Payment or Savings (2) x 50%	(4) Present-Value Factor @10%	(5) Present Value (2) or (3) x (4)
Cost	0	$10,000	$ —	1.000	$(10,000)
Depreciation	1	1,800	900	.909	818
Depreciation	2	1,800	900	.826	743
Depreciation	3	1,800	900	.751	676
Depreciation	4	1,800	900	.683	615
Depreciation	5	1,800	900	.621	559
Salvage Value	5	1,000		.621	621
					$(5,968)

Column (1) The estimated economic life is five years.
Column (2) The cost is $10,000. The estimated salvage value is $1,000. The depreciation for each of the five years is $1,800.

Explanation of Illustration 1

35

Column (3) The assumed tax rate is 50%. The estimated tax savings on the depreciation deduction for each of the five years is $900.

Column (4) The present-value factor for each year is the discounted value of $1 at 10% for that many years. For example, .909 can be invested now. At a 10% growth rate, the investor will have $1 in a year. Also, .826 can be invested now. At a 10% growth rate, the investor will have $1 in two years.

Column (5) The $10,000 cost is an outlay. Subtracted from this is (1) the present value of the tax benefits derived from the depreciation deductions, and (2) the present value of the salvage. The final figure is the estimated present-value cost of the asset if it is purchased.

ILLUSTRATION 2

LEASE ALTERNATIVE FOR THE DETERMINISTIC MODEL —

FIVE-YEAR LIFE

	(1) End of Year	(2) Amount	(3) Net After Tax Deduction (2) x (1 − .50)	(4) Present-Value Factor @ 10%	(5) Present Value (3) x (4)
Payments	1	$2,800	$1,400	.909	$(1,273)
Payments	2	2,800	1,400	.826	(1,156)
Payments	3	2,800	1,400	.751	(1,051)
Payments	4	2,800	1,400	.683	(956)
Payments	5	2,800	1,400	.621	(869)
					$(5,305)

Explanation of Illustration 2

Column (1) The lease period is five years.

Column (2) The yearly lease payments are $2,800.

Column (3) The tax rate is assumed to be 50%. The after-tax lease cost is $1,400 a year.

Column (4) The present-value factor for each year is the discounted value of $1 at 10% for that many years.

Column (5) The total estimated present-value cost of leasing is $5,305.

There are several inputs to the model that can be objectively determined. These include the cost, the depreciation method and the amount of the lease payments.

There are several inputs to the model that must be subjectively determined. These include the probable number of years of economic life of the investment, the actual salvage values given the number of years of life, the probable tax rate in each year of economic life and the appropriate discount rate.

By changing some of these inputs in the deterministic model, different present-value costs can be calculated. For example, if Illustration 1 contains a salvage value of $2,000 at the end of five years, the results are as shown in Illustration 3.

ILLUSTRATION 3
PURCHASE ALTERNATIVE FOR THE DETERMINISTIC MODEL—
TAX AND ACTUAL SALVAGE VALUE THE SAME

	(1) End of Year	(2) Amount	(3) Tax Payment or Savings (2) x 50%	(4) Present-Value Factor @ 10%	(5) Present Value (2) or (3) x (4)
Cost	0	$10,000		1.000	$(10,000)
Depreciation	1	1,600*	800	.909	727
Depreciation	2	1,600*	800	.826	661
Depreciation	3	1,600*	800	.751	601
Depreciation	4	1,600*	800	.683	546
Depreciation	5	1,600*	800	.621	497
Salvage Value	5	2,000		.621	1,242
					$(5,726)

*(10,000 — 2,000) x .20

Illustrations 1, 2 and 3 are useful if the investor is fairly certain of the economic life. Given all of the assumptions that the user makes about the cost, the tax rate, the rental terms, the discount rate, etc., he can easily tell which financing arrangement is more costly. The approximate cost savings of leasing or purchasing can be calculated according to the following formula.

1. Quantify the variables, such as the number of years of life, the depreciation method, the salvage value, the tax rate and the discount rate.
2. Set up a format similar to the one shown in Illustrations 1, 2 and 3.
3. Subtract the total present value of the lease alternative from the total present value of the purchase alternative.

By reference to Illustrations 1 and 2, the reader can see that approximately $663 can be saved by leasing if the asset is kept five years ($5,968 — $5,305).

It should be noted that these savings will accrue *only* if the assumptions listed in 1 above hold true. The user must supply appropriate figures.

The cost figure is not necessarily the invoice amount. The following illustration shows how other factors can be worked in.

DETERMINATION OF PURCHASE COST

Invoice cost of new asset	$10,000
Salvage value of old asset	(1,000)
Present value of maintenance charges or $450 a year for five years at 10%	1,705*
Present value of saved repairs on old asset — $1,000 in year 3	(751)
Cost for capital budgeting purposes	$ 9,954

*These would be paid separately if the asset were leased.

It is very important that the user have a general idea of the relative cost benefits of each financing method.

Studies by the General Accounting Office conducted several years ago showed that certain federal government agencies were, in some cases, "buying" computers through lease costs after a period of about two to three years. Because these government agencies used these computers for several years, several hundred thousand dollars were overspent.

If the reader feels that four years is a better estimate of the economic life of the asset, Illustration 4 is appropriate.

ILLUSTRATION 4
PURCHASE ALTERNATIVE FOR THE DETERMINISTIC MODEL—
FOUR-YEAR LIFE

	(1) End of Year	(2) Amount	(3) Tax Payment or Savings (2) x 50%	(4) Present-Value Factor @ 10%	(5) Present Value (2) or (3) x (4)
Cost	0	10,000	—	1.000	$(10,000)
Depreciation	1	1,900	950	.909	864
Depreciation	2	1,900	950	.826	785
Depreciation	3	1,900	950	.751	713
Depreciation	4	1,900	950	.683	649
Salvage Value	4	2,400		.683	1,639
					$(5,350)

The Probabilistic Model

By calculating a present-value cost for each probable economic life (three years, four years, etc.), the accountant can give management a distribution that will be more beneficial than one showing only a single estimated life. The value of the schedule can also be enhanced by assigning probabilities to each estimate of economic life. A possible distribution for the purchase alternative is shown in Illustration 5. The present-value amounts in column (2) are assumed figures. They are equivalent to the figures in column (5) of Illustrations 1-4.

This analysis is particularly valuable because it expresses the user's thinking on the subject. This is the best estimate of the present-value cost of purchasing and/or leasing.

ILLUSTRATION 5
A POSSIBLE PROBABILITY DISTRIBUTION FOR THE PURCHASE ALTERNATIVE

(1) No. of Years of Estimated Life	(2) Present Value	(3) Probability That Asset Will Be Used This Many Years	(4) Expected Net Present Value Cost (2) x (3)
3	$(5,000)	.20	$(1,000)
4	(5,500)	.30	(1,650)
5	(6,000)	.30	(1,800)
6	(6,500)	.20	(1,300)
			$(5,750)

ILLUSTRATION 6
INPUT FACTORS FOR THE PURCHASE ALTERNATIVE MODEL

	Estimate of Useful Life — In Years			
	3	4	5	6
Cost of Asset	$10,000			
Number of Estimates of Useful Life	4			
Salvage Value	2,000	$1,500	$1,000	$500
Tax Rate	.50	.50	.50	.50
Number of Years	3	4	5	6
Depreciation %	.333	.25	.20	.166
Present Value — Year 1	.909	.909	.909	.909
Depreciation %	.333	.25	.20	.166
Present Value — Year 2	.826	.826	.826	.826
Depreciation %	.333	.25	.20	.166
Present Value — Year 3	.751	.751	.751	.751
Depreciation %		.25	.20	.166
Present Value — Year 4		.683	.683	.683
Depreciation %			.20	.166
Present Value — Year 5			.621	.621
Depreciation %				.166
Present Value — Year 6				.564
Probability % for Each Year of Estimated Life	.10	.40	.40	.10

Using the model shown in Illustration 1, probability percentages are attached to the various estimates of useful life. The model is constructed so that the user can input any dollar amount that he considers appropriate.

Illustration 6 shows the amounts that are used for estimates of three, four, five and six years of useful life. A company using this model may input any amounts that it desires. Illustration 7 is an example of the output. Illustration 8 is the flowchart.

Calculation of the Present-Value Cost of Purchasing— With the Use of Probability

ILLUSTRATION 7
EXAMPLE OF OUTPUT GENERATED
BY THE PURCHASE ALTERNATIVE—
THE PROBABILITY MODEL

	(1) End of Year	(2) Amount	(3) Tax Payment or Savings (2) x 50%	(4) Present-Value Factor @ 10%	(5) Present Value (2) or (3) x (4)	(6) Proba- bility	(7) Expected Present Value (5) x (6)
			THREE-YEAR LIFE				
Cost	0	$10,000	$ —	1.000	$(10,000)		
Depreciation	1	2,666	1,333	.909	1,212		
Depreciation	2	2,666	1,333	.826	1,101		
Depreciation	3	2,666	1,333	.751	1,001		
Salvage Value	3	2,000	—	.751	1,502		
					$(5,184)	.10	$(518)
			FOUR-YEAR LIFE				
Cost	0	$10,000	$ —	1.000	$(10,000)		
Depreciation	1	2,125	1,063	.909	966		
Depreciation	2	2,125	1,063	.826	878		
Depreciation	3	2,125	1,063	.751	798		
Depreciation	4	2,125	1,063	.683	726		
Salvage Value	4	1,500	—	.683	1,025		
					$(5,607)	.40	$(2,243)

FIVE-YEAR LIFE

Cost	0	$10,000	$ —	1.000	$(10,000)
Depreciation	1	1,800	900	.909	818
Depreciation	2	1,800	900	.826	743
Depreciation	3	1,800	900	.751	676
Depreciation	4	1,800	900	.683	615
Depreciation	5	1,800	900	.621	559
Salvage Value	5	1,000	—	.621	621
					$(5,968)
				.40	$(2,387)

SIX-YEAR LIFE

Cost	0	$10,000	—	1.000	$(10,000)
Depreciation	1	1,583	792	.909	720
Depreciation	2	1,583	792	.826	654
Depreciation	3	1,583	792	.751	595
Depreciation	4	1,583	792	.683	541
Depreciation	5	1,583	792	.621	492
Depreciation	6	1,583	792	.564	447
Salvage Value	6	500	—	.564	282
					$(6,269)
				.10	$(627)
					$(5,775)

Step 1. Determine:
   (A) The purchase cost—example in top figure in column (2), Illustration 7.
   (B) The number of estimates of economic life—four.
   (C) The probability of each estimate—example in column (6), Illustration 7.

Step 2. Estimate the actual salvage value—example in column (2), Illustration 7.

Step 3. Introduce the tax rate—50%.

Step 4. Determine the depreciable amount—the cost in column (2), Illustration 7 minus the salvage value in column (2), Illustration 7.

Step 5. Calculate depreciation—step 4 amount times depreciation percentage—result in column (2), Illustration 7.

Step 6. Calculate tax benefit on depreciation—step 5 times step 3—result in column (3), Illustration 7.

Step 7. Calculate the present value of the tax benefit on depreciation—step 6 times present-value percentage in column (4)—result in column (5), Illustration 7.

Step 8. Add step 7 amount to total—repeat steps 5-7 for each year.

Step 9. Calculate the present value of the estimated salvage— multiply the step 2 amount times the present-value percentage—result in column (5), Illustration 7.

Step 10. Calculate the present-value cost of purchasing—add up all amounts in column (5), Illustration 7.

Step 11. Calculate expected present value—multiply total of column (5), Illustration 7, times column (6), Illustration 7—result in column (7), Illustration 7. Add step 11 amount to total.

Step 12. Repeat steps 2-11 for each estimated life.

Step 13. Determine the grand total of the expected present-value costs—result at the bottom of column (7), Illustration 7.

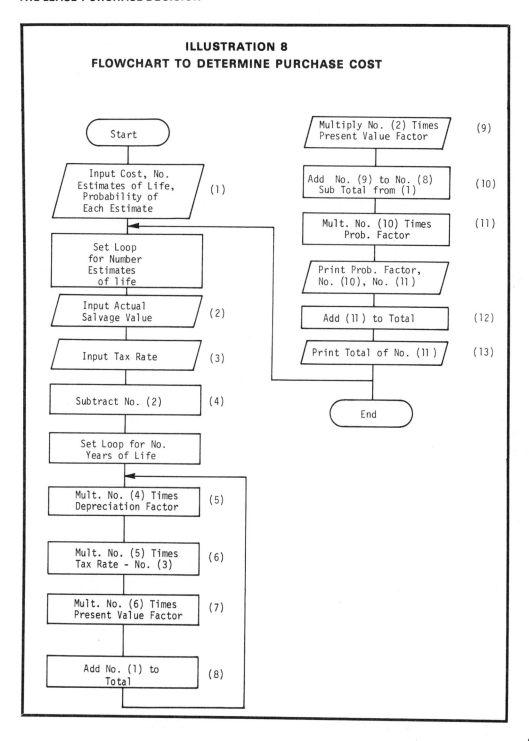

ILLUSTRATION 8
FLOWCHART TO DETERMINE PURCHASE COST

Start

Input Cost, No. Estimates of Life, Probability of Each Estimate (1)

Set Loop for Number Estimates of life

Input Actual Salvage Value (2)

Input Tax Rate (3)

Subtract No. (2) (4)

Set Loop for No. Years of Life

Mult. No. (4) Times Depreciation Factor (5)

Mult. No. (5) Times Tax Rate - No. (3) (6)

Mult. No. (6) Times Present Value Factor (7)

Add No. (1) to Total (8)

Multiply No. (2) Times Present Value Factor (9)

Add No. (9) to No. (8) Sub Total from (1) (10)

Mult. No. (10) Times Prob. Factor (11)

Print Prob. Factor, No. (10), No. (11)

Add (11) to Total (12)

Print Total of No. (11) (13)

End

45

Calculation of the Present-Value Cost of Leasing— With the Use of Probability

The model shown in Illustration 2 can be used to calculate the expected present-value cost of leasing. A step-by-step explanation is given below.

Step 1. Determine the yearly lease payment—amount in column (2), Illustration 10.

Step 2. Calculate the after-tax lease cost—multiply the amount in column (2), Illustration 10 times 1 minus the tax rate—result in column (3), Illustration 10.

Step 3. Calculate the present value of the lease cost—column (3), Illustration 10 times column 4, Illustration 10—result in column (5), Illustration 10.

Step 4. Calculate the expected present-value cost—multiply the amount in column (5), Illustration 10 times the amount in column (6), Illustration 10—result in column (7), Illustration 10.

Step 5. Add column (7) amounts to total.

Step 6. Repeat steps 2-5 for each estimate of useful life.

Step 7. Determine the grand total of expected present-value costs.

Illustration 9 is a table showing the amounts that are used for estimates of three, four, five and six years of useful life. Illustration 10 is the output.

ILLUSTRATION 9
INPUT FACTORS FOR THE LEASE ALTERNATIVE MODEL

	Estimate of Useful Life in Years			
	3	4	5	6
Lease Payments	$2,800			
1 — Tax Rate	.50			
Number of Estimates of Useful Life	4			
Present Value	2.486	3.169	3.790	4.354
Probability Percentage for Each Year of Estimated Life	.10	.40	.40	.10

ILLUSTRATION 10

OUTPUT FOR THE LEASE ALTERNATIVE MODEL

	(1) End of Year	(2) Yearly Amount	(3) Net After Tax (2) x (1 minus .50)	(4) Present-Value Factor @ 10%*
3-Year Life Payments	3	$2,800	$1,400	2.486
4-Year Life Payments	4	2,800	1,400	3.169
5-Year Life Payments	5	2,800	1,400	3.790
6-Year Life Payments	6	2,800	1,400	4.354

	(5) Present-Value Cost (2) or (3) x (4)	(6) Proba- bility	(7) Expected Present- Value Cost
3-Year Life Payments	$(3,480)	.10	$ (348)
4-Year Life Payments	(4,437)	.40	(1,775)
5-Year Life Payments	(5,306)	.40	(2,122)
6-Year Life Payments	(6,096)	.10	(610)
			$(4,855)

*Because the yearly lease payments are assumed to be the same, the present-value factors for all years are summed and one multiplication is performed.

The bottom part of Illustration 7 (the purchase alternative) and the bottom part of Illustration 10 (the lease alternative) are repeated in Illustration 12.

Analysis of the Models

1. There is a small chance (10 percent) that substantial money will be saved by leasing (three years, $5,184 — $3,480 = $1,704).
2. There is a little less than a 50-50 chance (40 percent) that $1,170 will be saved if the asset is leased (four years, $5,607 — $4,437).
3. The user can expect to save about $920 ($5,775 — $4,855) by leasing the asset. If there are some special features of leasing or purchasing that make one of these methods especially attractive, these features can be worked into the model.

47

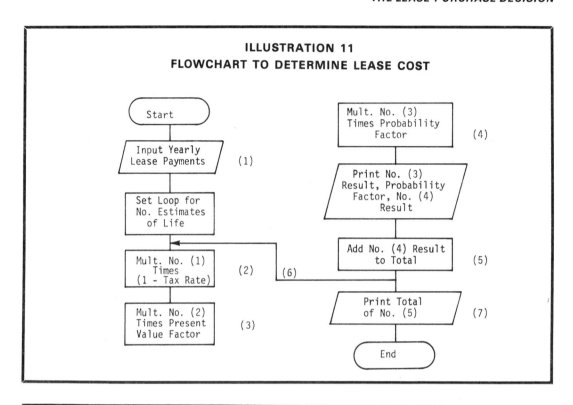

ILLUSTRATION 11
FLOWCHART TO DETERMINE LEASE COST

ILLUSTRATION 12
COMPARISON OF PURCHASE AND
LEASE MODELS

	Present-Value Cost of Purchasing	Present-Value Cost of Leasing	Expected Present-Value Cost of Purchasing	Expected Present-Value Cost of Leasing	Probability
3-Year Life	$(5,184)	$(3,480)	$(518)	$(348)	.10
4-Year Life	(5,607)	(4,437)	(2,243)	(1,775)	.40
5-Year Life	(5,968)	(5,306)	(2,387)	(2,122)	.40
6-Year Life	(6,269)	(6,096)	(627)	(610)	.10
			$(5,775)	$(4,855)	

Summary Comments

The advantage of the models illustrated in this chapter is their flexibility. The user can input whatever numerical factors are appropriate to his situation and come out with a cost savings figure.

3

The Use of Probability in Setting Control Limits for Variances from Standards

Standard cost systems may be employed by organizations for a variety of reasons. Most accountants will agree, however, that a major benefit of such a system is cost control (keeping costs within tolerable limits). For this reason, a variety of variances have been derived for the purpose of spotlighting and correcting deviations from the standard.

Variance analysis is of limited use, however, unless some distinction can be made between the deviations that need investigation and those that are "random" in nature. To elaborate on this point, it is necessary to explain the basis upon which many standards are calculated. Illustration 1 contains a sample of labor hours that could be used to establish a budget.

The sample distribution in the following illustration is reasonably close to normal because the mean, median and mode are about the same (between 23 and 24). The standard hours that should be used to complete this particular job or project is 23.24. In this case, the standard is an average of averages derived from previously observed hourly totals.

ILLUSTRATION 1
AN EXAMPLE OF HOW A SAMPLE
OF ACTUAL LABOR HOURS COULD
BE USED TO ESTABLISH A STANDARD

Studies might be made on how long it takes to perform a certain job or to finish a certain project. A tally of the actual hours would be made and an average formulated. In effect, this average would be the standard upon which future labor-hour performance would be judged. The following example illustrates the use of a set of four daily tallies to create one sample. The total sample size is nine.

Tally	Number of Hours				Average
	1	2	3	4	
Day 1	18.80	22.00	21.00	24.00	21.45
Day 2	19.00	19.00	21.00	23.00	20.50
Day 3	24.00	23.00	22.00	24.60	23.40
Day 4	19.50	23.60	22.00	21.90	21.75
Day 5	25.00	22.10	22.50	24.80	23.60
Day 6	26.70	22.50	24.50	24.30	24.50
Day 7	28.60	25.00	26.80	26.80	26.80
Day 8	19.50	24.20	22.20	26.10	23.00
Day 9	25.50	20.00	23.50	27.80	24.20
Total					209.20
Average of Averages					23.24

The Desirability of Separating Random and Nonrandom Deviations

Obviously, production personnel do not expect every daily average of hours to coincide with the standard of 23.24. However, they do feel that the daily tally of hours should be within tolerable limits. If this tally is out of control, investigation should be made and corrective action taken. These officials also recognize that needless investigation of deviations will be costly and time consuming. Therefore, the problem is to decide what control limits should be set around the standard of 23.24 hours. Any daily average of hours that falls within the control limits will be considered a random variance and will be ignored. On the other hand, averages outside the prescribed boundaries will be checked out and, if possible, corrective action taken.

The Standard Deviation

If the sample distribution that is used to construct the standard is normal, statistical theory can be applied to the numbers in order to set reasonable control limits. Illustration 2 contains a calculation of the standard deviation of the average in Illustration 1.

In a normal distribution, approximately 68 percent of the elements will fall within $\pm$ 1 standard deviation from the average of that distribution. Illustration 3 shows the average and $\pm$ 1 standard deviation.

ILLUSTRATION 2
CALCULATION OF THE STANDARD
DEVIATION OF THE AVERAGES
IN ILLUSTRATION 1

(1) Average of Averages	(2) Averages	(3) (1) − (2) Deviations	(4) (3) x (3) Deviations Squared
23.24	21.45	1.79	3.20
23.24	20.50	2.74	7.51
23.24	23.40	.16	.03
23.24	21.75	1.49	2.22
23.24	23.60	.36	.13
23.24	24.50	1.26	1.59
23.24	26.80	3.56	12.67
23.24	23.00	.24	.06
23.24	24.20	.96	.92

Deviations Total   28.33

Deviations Total divided by 8
(the sample size minus 1)*   3.54

The Square Root is (rounded off)   1.88

*Standard deviation of a sample is biased downward in relation to the standard deviation of a population. Because the purpose of taking this sample is to estimate population characteristics, the denominator is lowered in order to take away this downward bias.

ILLUSTRATION 3
A DISTRIBUTION OF THE
AVERAGES IN ILLUSTRATION 2—
23.24 ± 1 STANDARD DEVIATION

23.24 Minus 1 Standard Deviation	Averages from Illustration 2 That Fall Within the Range	23.24 Plus 1 Standard Deviation
23.24 − 1.88 = 21.36	21.45 23.40 21.75 23.60 24.50 23.00 24.20	23.24 + 1.88 = 25.12

By reference to Illustration 2, it can be seen that seven of the nine examples are within ± 1 standard deviation of the mean.

This, of course, is higher than 68 percent because of the small size and the discrete nature of the distribution. The 21.45 sample is barely within range. If the amount were slightly smaller, it would probably fall outside the range leaving six out of nine (67 percent) within the limits.

Another characteristic of the normal distribution is that approximately 90 percent of the observations will fall within ± 1.64 standard deviations of the average of that distribution. Illustration 4 also shows this.

ILLUSTRATION 4
A DISTRIBUTION OF THE
AVERAGES IN ILLUSTRATION 2—
23.24 ± STANDARD DEVIATIONS

23.24 − 1.64 Standard Deviations	Averages from Illustration 2 That Fall Within the Range			23.24 + 1.64 Standard Deviations
23.24 − (1.88 x 1.64) = 20.16	21.45	20.50	23.40	23.24 + (1.88 x 1.64) = 26.32
	21.75	23.60	24.50	
	23.00	24.20		

In Illustration 4 the range includes eight of nine samples or 88 percent (fairly close to 90 percent). Statistical tables are available that indicate the various percentages associated with certain multiples of the standard deviation. As the percentage becomes larger, the range widens.*

Use of Control Limits

The company or consulting accountant can make use of these statistical measures to set appropriate control limits. Once these limits are set, the daily hourly averages that fall below or above the designated control limits will be automatically checked. Those figures that are "in bounds" will be ignored.

---

*Some percentages and multiples are:

68% = 1.00	95% = 1.96
80% = 1.28	96% = 2.00
90% = 1.64	99% + = 3.00

The accountant's task is to decide what percentage of the observations should be included within the control area. A number of factors should be considered.

1. Prior experience may reveal that approximately 5 percent of the time the investigation of high variances uncovered a discrepancy, such as a faulty machine or inexperienced labor. About 5 percent of the time, variance investigation showed that an unusually low hourly total was due to the efficiency of the work force. The rest of the time variance checks proved to be groundless, i.e., no apparent cause existed for the differences. Thus, the control limits could be set at 90 percent, which means that all hourly deviations ± 1.64 standard deviations from the standard will be ignored. Of course, a 10 percent risk is being taken that variances will be needlessly investigated since it is possible that *all* deviations are random.

2. A factor that should also be considered is the cost of investigating versus the cost of not investigating. For example, assume that the labor function is an assembly process and that hourly averages that are "out of control" must be checked out and reported on by the department supervisor. If the firm feels that diverted time is a cost (there is good reason to take this position), the supervisor's average pay rate for the investigation period is considered the burden. Likewise, there is probably a cost associated with ignoring deviations that prove later to be significant and nonrandom. Too many hours may be spent assembling a product as a result of poor machinery. This can cause excessive costs or a poor-quality product that suffers in the market place.

3. The nature of the product or service is significant. Management will be somewhat conservative and set tight limits on the assembly of "critical" items (certain medical supplies, for example). The needless investigation of this type of product is important, but the failure to investigate when it is called for is even more critical.

Factors to Be Considered in Setting the Control Limits

A Step-by-Step Approach in Setting Control Limits

STEP 1. DECIDE WHAT TYPE OF DATA WILL BE USED TO SET THE STANDARD.

The use of historical information is popular in industry, and this particular method is used earlier in the chapter. A variation of this technique is to adjust historical data for anticipated changes in the future. For example, the purchase of new machinery might improve a labor routine so that the standard hours for performing a function with this machinery is lowered.

STEP 2. GATHER THE DATA THAT WILL BE USED TO SET THE STANDARD.

Enough samples should be collected so that the distribution is approximately normal. If the population of the data (labor hours, for example) is normal, a sample similar to the one shown in Illustration 1 might be sufficient. If the population is skewed (extreme elements exist), a larger sample size will probably be necessary. The accountant should be on guard for items that are atypical and that need to be thrown out. Assume that the data gathered in Illustration 1 contain a daily average of 35.00 hours. This figure is clearly out of line with the rest of the daily averages. Inclusion of this amount will create an upward bias in the standard and the result will be upper control limits that are too high. Investigation might show that on that particular day temporary employees were assembling the product. In this case, the 35.00 should not be included in the tally of daily averages. Instead, this figure can be treated as a separate variance. The only other way to overcome extreme values of this type is to increase the size of the sample, which, of course, is time consuming.

STEP 3. COMPUTE THE AVERAGE AND THE STANDARD DEVIATION OF THE ELEMENTS THAT MAKE UP THE STANDARD.

This procedure is demonstrated in Illustration 2. The use of the sample size minus one to obtain the standard deviation is due to the fact that samples are being used rather than the entire population. The standard deviation is 1.88 hours.

STEP 4. DECIDE WHAT MULTIPLE OF THE STANDARD DEVIATION SHOULD BE USED TO SET THE CONTROL LIMITS.

This decision is a matter of judgment. It is possible that the same limits will be used until some evidence is obtained that shows new percentages should be calculated.

STEP 5. COMPUTE THE UPPER AND LOWER CONTROL LIMITS.

Illustrations 3 and 4 show how this is done with ± 1 standard deviation and ± 1.64 standard deviations, respectively. Illustration 5 shows the control limits that would be set with a variety of standard deviation multiples.

ILLUSTRATION 5
DETERMINATION OF CONTROL
LIMITS USING SEVERAL
MULTIPLES OF THE STANDARD DEVIATION

Standard	Standard Deviation	Control Limit %	Standard Deviation Multiple	Limits[1]	Limits[2]
23.24 hours	1.88 hours	65	.93	24.99 hours	21.49 hours
23.24 hours	1.88 hours	70	1.04	25.20 hours	21.28 hours
23.24 hours	1.88 hours	75	1.15	25.40 hours	21.08 hours
23.24 hours	1.88 hours	80	1.28	25.65 hours	20.83 hours
23.24 hours	1.88 hours	85	1.44	25.95 hours	20.53 hours
23.24 hours	1.88 hours	90	1.64	26.32 hours	20.16 hours
23.24 hours	1.88 hours	95	1.96	26.92 hours	19.56 hours
23.24 hours	1.88 hours	99	2.58	28.09 hours	18.39 hours

[1]23.24 + (1.88 x appropriate multiple)
[2]23.24 − (1.88 x appropriate multiple)

The versatility of this model is that the accountant can input any multiple of the standard deviation that he chooses and a different set of control limits will be obtained. A table similar to the one shown in Illustration 5 can be generated (with or without a computer). On the basis of this table, a decision can then be reached on the proper limits.

STEP 6. DECIDE WHICH AMOUNTS FALL INSIDE AND OUTSIDE THE RANGE OF THE CONTROL LIMITS.

Once the dollar boundaries are set, this decision becomes routine. Occasionally the user may wish to look at the deviation that falls within the prescribed limits. This would be done only for special reasons, however.

Flowchart to Demonstrate Previous Steps

The flowchart, Illustration 6, shows the steps explained in the previous section.

Control Limits for Flexible Budget Variances

All of the examples in previous sections of this chapter deal with control limits around a single figure. This is appropriate when the subject matter is materials or labor. Overhead standards (usually called budgets) are flexible, however. A different figure is supplied for each anticipated level of activity. While material and labor standards are usually expressed in unit or hourly amounts, the overhead flexible budget is generally shown as a dollar total.

Assume, for illustrative purposes, that the flexible budget for repair costs is:

$1,000 (Fixed Cost) + $.50 x (Number of Machine Hours)*

---

*Chapter 4 contains a detailed description of a statistical technique used to derive a flexible budget.

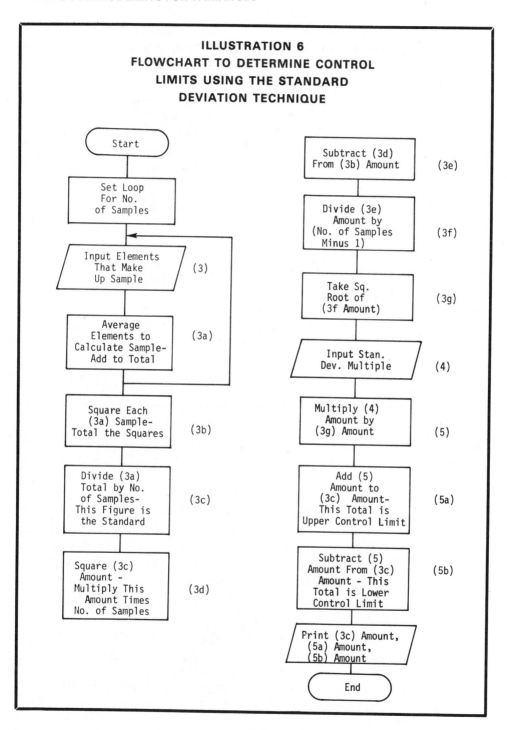

ILLUSTRATION 6
FLOWCHART TO DETERMINE CONTROL
LIMITS USING THE STANDARD
DEVIATION TECHNIQUE

Start

Set Loop
For No.
of Samples

Input Elements
That Make
Up Sample   (3)

Average
Elements to
Calculate Sample-   (3a)
Add to Total

Square Each
(3a) Sample-
Total the Squares   (3b)

Divide (3a)
Total by No.
of Samples-   (3c)
This Figure is
the Standard

Square (3c)
Amount -
Multiply This   (3d)
Amount Times
No. of Samples

Subtract (3d)
From (3b) Amount   (3e)

Divide (3e)
Amount by
(No. of Samples   (3f)
Minus 1)

Take Sq.
Root of   (3g)
(3f Amount)

Input Stan.
Dev. Multiple   (4)

Multiply (4)
Amount by
(3g) Amount   (5)

Add (5)
Amount to
(3c)   Amount-   (5a)
This Total is
Upper Control Limit

Subtract (5)
Amount From (3c)   (5b)
Amount - This
Total is Lower
Control Limit

Print (3c) Amount,
(5a) Amount,
(5b) Amount

End

Illustration 7 shows the budget or standard cost at each anticipated machine hour level. Hypothetical actual costs are also shown.

ILLUSTRATION 7
EXAMPLE OF A FLEXIBLE BUDGET

Machine Hours	Actual Repair Costs	Budgeted or Standard Repair Costs[*]	Difference
1,000	$1,420	$1,500	$(80)
1,100	1,470	1,550	(80)
1,200	1,490	1,600	(110)
1,300	1,600	1,650	(50)
1,400	1,730	1,700	30
1,500	1,790	1,750	40
1,600	1,880	1,800	80
1,700	1,900	1,850	50
1,800	1,980	1,900	80

*$1,000 + $.50 x (Number of Machine Hours)

The budget formula is derived from the actual costs. If this sample of actual costs is approximately normal in distribution, the usual statements can be made about the dispersion of these costs around the arithmetic mean. The only difference is in the method that is used to calculate the standard deviation (technically called the standard error of the estimate in this case). Each flexible budget figure represents a type of arithmetic mean. Therefore, the standard deviation is calculated according to Illustration 8.

If 90 percent control limits were set, the upper and lower control limits shown in Illustration 9 would be set. Notice that the multiple of the standard deviation is added to and subtracted from *each* different flexible budget figure.

All of the actual repair costs at each machine hour level fall within range. The use of this type of control limit calls for a

ILLUSTRATION 8
CALCULATION OF THE STANDARD
DEVIATION OF THE FLEXIBLE
BUDGET FIGURES IN
ILLUSTRATION 7

Differences Between Actual and Budget Costs — from Illustration 7	Differences Squared
$(80)	$ 6,400
(80)	6,400
(110)	12,100
(50)	2,500
30	900
40	1,600
80	6,400
50	2,500
80	6,400
	$45,200 ÷ 7* = $6,457. Square Root = $80.36

*Statisticians suggest the use of the sample size minus 2 for this type of measurement.

ILLUSTRATION 9
CALCULATION OF CONTROL LIMITS
AROUND THE FLEXIBLE BUDGET
DATA IN ILLUSTRATION 7—
90 PERCENT CONTROL LIMITS

(1) Flexible Budget Amounts from Illustration 7	(2) Upper Control Limit — [($80.36 x 1.64) + Column (1)]	(3) Lower Control Limit — [($80.36 x 1.64) − Column (1)]	(4) Actual Repair Costs from Illustration 7
$1,500.00	$1,631.79	$1,368.21	$1,420.00
1,550.00	1,681.79	1,418.21	1,470.00
1,600.00	1,731.79	1,468.21	1,490.00
1,650.00	1,781.79	1,518.21	1,600.00
1,700.00	1,831.79	1,568.21	1,730.00
1,750.00	1,881.79	1,618.21	1,790.00
1,800.00	1,931.79	1,668.21	1,880.00
1,850.00	1,981.79	1,718.21	1,900.00
1,900.00	2,031.79	1,768.21	1,980.00

different set of upper and lower limits for each different activity level. These limits can be used by the accountant to measure the acceptability of repair costs every time a certain activity level is achieved. For example, the use of 1,200 machine hours will automatically call for a repair budget of $1,600. However, any actual repair cost between $1,468.21 and $1,731.79 will be accepted as a random variation and will not be investigated. Any actual repair cost lower than $1,468.21 or higher than $1,731.79 will be analyzed for causes and possible corrective action.

Summary and Critique

The internal or consulting accountant can benefit from employing the statistical devices described in this chapter. However, judgment should be used when necessary. For example, it may become apparent that some permanent change has taken place in the population due to excessive variations that continue period after period. Instead of routinely investigating this type of variance, some thought should be given to calculating a new standard.

4

The Use of the Least Squares Technique to Determine the Pattern of Revenues and Costs

Regression and correlation analysis is used by a number of **Introduction**
business enterprises. The Upjohn Company, Kalamazoo,
Michigan, made a study of the historical relationship between
direct expense and the number of salesmen for a four-month
period. The data were plotted and a regression line was
calculated. Using the regression line as a budget forecast, the
actual direct expenses were compared with the budget
figures.*

Two methods, however, have been traditionally used to
budget company costs:

1. The "intuitive" approach in which prior periods'
   historical costs are adjusted for anticipated changes in
   future periods.
2. Some variation of the high-low approach in which
   aggregate linear relationships are used. For example, assume that machine repair costs and machine hours are as
   shown in shown in Illustration 1.

The January 19X1 machine hours figure is the lowest
observed level of activity during the accounting period. The
June 19X1 figure is the highest during the same period. A
3,000 change in machine hours is divided into a cor-
responding $600 change in repair costs. The result is $.20.
The $.20 is then multiplied by 5,000 machine hours and sub-
tracted from $2,000 to arrive at the fixed portion of the cost.
The derived budget formula is:

$$\$1,000 + \$.20 \text{ per machine hour.}$$

*Bradley, Hugh E., "Setting and Controlling Budgets with Regression
Analysis," *Management Accounting,* November, 1969, pp. 31-34.

```
┌─────────────────────────────────────────────────────┐
│                   ILLUSTRATION 1                      │
│         DETERMINATION OF THE VARIABILITY              │
│         OF MACHINE REPAIR COSTS USING                 │
│               THE HIGH-LOW METHOD                     │
│                                                       │
│   Time Period      Machine Hours    Repair Costs      │
│   ─────────────────────────────────────────────────  │
│   January, 19X1        5,000          $2,000          │
│   June, 19X1           8,000           2,600          │
└─────────────────────────────────────────────────────┘
```

Appraisal of the Traditional Methods

The intuitive method may be applicable when prior costs have no discernible pattern. However, this approach can also be needlessly time consuming for costs that do have some linearity.

The high-low method is easy to calculate and to apply, but it makes too much use of aggregate relationships. The fact that a cost pattern is linear from its low point to its high point does not ensure that the pattern is linear throughout. Nor is this any assurance that the cost pattern in the future will have the same degree of linearity. The high-low method does not provide enough evidence. The sample size is not large enough.

Accountants can render their organization or their clients service by suggesting the use of more sophisticated statistical techniques for budgeting certain costs. Much of the time-saving convenience of the high-low method is retained and a more scientifically sound basis for budgeting is established. In addition to this, a great amount of time and expense can be saved later by avoiding unnecessary investigations of budget variations.

The Application of the Least Squares Technique— Correlation with Activity

The least squares technique is a statistical device for fitting a linear or straight line to a series of numbers. It is, in effect, an average. The least squares method minimizes the squares of the deviations of the data from the straight line and is thus the line of "best fit."

The formula for this straight line is familiar:

$$y = a + bx$$

where y is the total cost, a is the fixed portion of the cost, b is the variable cost per unit, hour, etc., and x is the level of activity.

Assume that accountants, as architects of the financial reporting system, are actively involved in the process of formulating a flexible budget. The purpose of this budget is to project into the future the amount of variable and semi-variable costs. The following steps should be taken for each applicable account.

STEP 1. DECIDE WHAT TYPE OF ACTIVITY SHOULD BE USED TO CORRELATE WITH THE ACCOUNT.

Often, there is one type of activity that causes the cost to change. For example, direct material and direct labor might increase proportionately as the number of manufactured units increases. In this example, repair costs are correlated to the number of machine hours used.

STEP 2. LIST THE MACHINE HOURS USED AND THE RELATED REPAIR COST FOR EACH APPROPRIATE TIME PERIOD.

The time periods can be months or years depending on the judgment of the accountants and the amount of data that is available. The use of months will provide *less* aggregate data and will probably prove to be more reliable. The number of periods should be enough to give a meaningful average. Care should be taken not to pick up outdated cost relationships. A material change in rates charged by repairmen could distort the results if costs under the old and new rate are included. If possible, the data should form a distribution that is fairly close to normal. If this is done, the user of the data will be able to predict the percentage of elements that will cluster around the average.

STEP 3. SQUARE EACH PERIOD'S MACHINE HOUR FIGURE. MULTIPLY EACH PERIOD'S MACHINE HOUR FIGURE TIMES EACH PERIOD'S REPAIR COST. LIST BOTH SETS OF FIGURES.

67

Illustration 2 shows the results of steps 2 and 3.

ILLUSTRATION 2
INFORMATION FOR THE CALCULATION
OF A REGRESSION LINE USING
THE LEAST SQUARES METHOD—
ASSUMING GOOD CORRELATION

Period	Total Machine Hours x	Repair Cost y	x^2	x y
1	10,019	$ 78	$ 100,380,361	$ 781,482
2	11,904	94	141,705,216	1,118,976
3	13,638	110	185,995,044	1,500,180
4	15,622	127	244,046,884	1,983,994
5	19,431	151	377,563,761	2,934,081
6	22,774	175	518,655,076	3,985,450
7	26,058	183	679,019,364	4,768,614
8	31,354	210	983,073,316	6,584,340
9	35,900	255	1,288,810,000	9,154,500
10	41,895	317	1,755,191,025	13,280,715
	228,595	1,700	$6,274,440,047	$46,092,332

There are two standard formulas that are used to calculate the regression line. They are:

1. $y = N(a) + x(b)$
2. $xy = x(a) + x^2(b)$

After substituting numbers from Illustration 2, the formulas read:

1. $\$1,700 = 10(a) + 228,595(b)$
2. $46,092,332 = 228,595(a) + 6,274,440,047(b)$

The reader need not give any attention to the manner in which the formulas are derived. The important thing is to understand the objective of the formulas. There are a number of ways that the two formulas can be solved. One method is the one in step 4.

STEP 4. MULTIPLY FORMULA 1 BY 22,859.5 IN ORDER TO MAKE THE VALUE OF (a) THE SAME IN BOTH FORMULAS.

Result 1.   38,861,150 = 228,595(a) + 5,225,567,403(b)
Result 2.   46,092,332 = 228,595(a) + 6,274,440,047(b)

STEP 5. SUBTRACT FORMULA 1 FROM FORMULA 2 IN ORDER TO "CLEAR OUT" (a).

Result: 7,231,182 = 1,048,872,644(b)

STEP 6. SOLVE THE RESULTING FORMULA FOR THE VALUE OF (b).

Result: $b = \dfrac{7,231,182}{1,048,872,644}$

   b = .007 (the variable cost)

STEP 7. SUBSTITUTE THE CALCULATED VALUE OF (b) BACK IN FORMULA 1 AND SOLVE FOR (a).

Result: $1,700 = $10(a) + 228,595 (.007)
          1,700 = $10(a) + 1,600
           10a = $100
            a = $10 (the fixed cost)

The formula for repair cost is $10 + .007 (the number of hours used).

Once the regression line has been calculated, there are *two* basic uses for it.

The Meaning of the Regression Line

1. An historical budget for (repair) costs can be formulated. For example, if the total machine hours used is 40,000 for a given accounting period, the budget for repair cost is:

   $10 + .007 (40,000) = $290

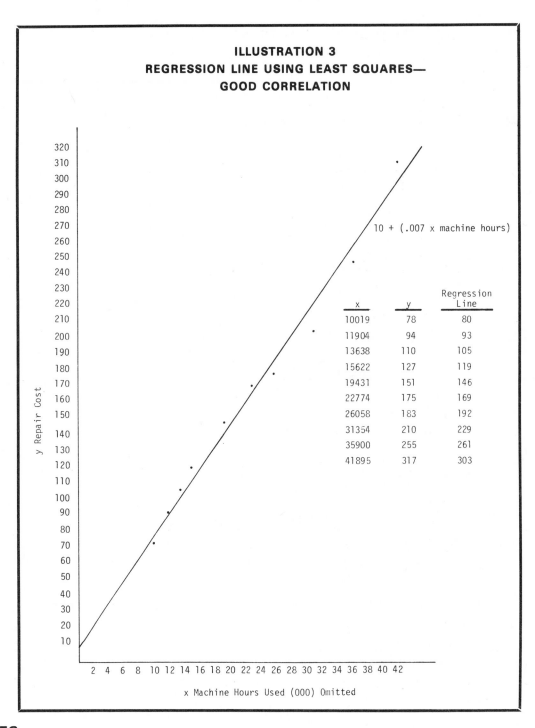

ILLUSTRATION 3
REGRESSION LINE USING LEAST SQUARES—
GOOD CORRELATION

10 + (.007 x machine hours)

x	y	Regression Line
10019	78	80
11904	94	93
13638	110	105
15622	127	119
19431	151	146
22774	175	169
26058	183	192
31354	210	229
35900	255	261
41895	317	303

y Repair Cost

x Machine Hours Used (000) Omitted

This figure cannot be supplied until the total machine hours are tabulated.

2. Repair costs in future accounting periods can be forecast. In order to do this accurately, valid forecasting methods must be developed for future machine hour usage.

Illustration 3 shows Illustration 2 data in plotted form. Note the closeness of the plotted actual costs to the straight line.

If there is some uncertainty as to whether good correlation exists, an additional statistical ratio can be calculated. This ratio measures the relative dispersion of the plotted actual figures around the regression line. A straight line can be plotted through almost any set of figures. Unless there is fairly good correlation between the two sets of figures, the projection shown by this straight line can be very misleading. In order to avoid this possible mistake, the following steps can be taken.

Proof of Correlation—the Coefficient of Determination

STEP 1. USING THE REGRESSION LINE DEVELOPED IN THE PREVIOUS SECTION, CALCULATE AND LIST THE ESTIMATED REPAIR COST FOR EACH OF THE TEN PERIODS.

STEP 2. CALCULATE AND LIST THE AVERAGE REPAIR COSTS FOR THE SAME TEN-YEAR PERIOD. ILLUSTRATION 4 SHOWS THESE DATA.

STEP 3. CALCULATE THE VARIANCE OF THE ACTUAL EXPENSES FROM THE ESTIMATED EXPENSES (REGRESSION LINE).

The variance is generally considered to be the best statistical measure of dispersion around the average. If the dispersion of the actual costs around the regression line is large, then the correlation is not very good.

ILLUSTRATION 4
DATA FOR CALCULATION OF THE COEFFICIENT OF DETERMINATION — GOOD CORRELATION

(1) Period	(2) Total Machine Hours Used	(3) Actual Repair Cost	(4) Estimated Cost— Regression Line	(5) Average Repair Cost Total of (3) ÷ 10	(6) Actual Minus Estimated (3) − (4)	(7) Actual Minus Average (3) − (5)
1	$ 10,019	$ 78	$ 80*	$ 170	$(2)	$(92)
2	11,904	94	93*	170	1	(76)
3	13,638	110	105*	170	5	(60)
4	15,622	127	119*	170	8	(43)
5	19,431	151	146*	170	5	(19)
6	22,774	175	169*	170	6	5
7	26,058	183	192*	170	(9)	13
8	31,354	210	229*	170	(19)	40
9	35,900	255	261*	170	(6)	85
10	41,895	317	303*	170	14	147
	$228,595	$1,700	$1,697	$1,700		

*$10 + .007 (machine hours used)

STEP 4. CALCULATE THE VARIANCE OF THE ACTUAL EXPENSES FROM THE AVERAGE EXPENSE.

The purpose of step 4 is to provide a basis for measuring the relative size of the variance calculated in step 3. It is obvious that the variance in step 4 will generally be larger. If the step 3 variance is almost as large as the step 4 variance, the correlation is not good. Another way to phrase the comparison is to say that if the regression line is similar to the average actual expense, the regression line loses its significance. The reason for this statement is that the average actual expense has little significance as a projection device.

Illustration 5 contains the necessary calculations for steps 3 and 4.

ILLUSTRATION 5
CALCULATION OF THE
COEFFICIENT OF DETERMINATION—
GOOD CORRELATION

(1)	(2) Actual Cost Minus Estimated Cost	(3) Column (2) Squared	(4) Actual Cost Minus Average Cost	(5) Column (4) Squared
Period				
1	$(2)	$ 4	$(92)	$ 8,464
2	1	1	(76)	5,776
3	5	25	(60)	3,600
4	8	64	(43)	1,849
5	5	25	(19)	361
6	6	36	5	25
7	(9)	81	13	169
8	(19)	361	40	1,600
9	(6)	36	85	7,225
10	14	196	147	21,609
		$829		$50,678
÷ (n − 2)		8		8
=		$104		$ 6,335

STEP 5. DIVIDE THE VARIANCE IN STEP 3 BY THE VARIANCE IN STEP 4. SUBTRACT THE RESULT FROM 1.

Result: Coefficient of Determination $= 1 - \dfrac{104}{6335} = .98$

At this point, the accountant must make a judgment as to whether the percentage represents sufficient correlation. The higher the percentage, the better the correlation. If time is available and it is considered desirable, a comparison can be made between the correlation of repair costs with machine hours used and the correlation of repair costs with some other type of activity.

Comparison of the Least Squares Method and the "Intuitive" Method

Although "intuitive" budgeting may appear to be less time consuming, the follow-up action taken with this approach may prove to be more time consuming in the long run. Illustration 4 shows differences between the actual and estimated costs. Note that in most cases the difference is fairly small. If these regression line figures had been used as budget figures during these ten periods, it is unlikely that many (if any) budget investigations would have been made.

On the other hand, the use of intuitive budgeting during the same ten periods might have and probably would have led to needless and costly budget investigation. The least squares method is a relatively easy statistical technique. If future cost patterns are expected to be as stable as past cost patterns, this device will produce budget projections that minimize deviations.

Poor Correlation

Proper care must be taken not to misuse the least squares method. Even if two sets of figures have little correlation, a straight line can be calculated that minimizes the deviations from that line. Budget projections based on this line, however, are not only useless but are misleading as well. Illustration 6 is an example of data that have poor correlation.

Least Squares Technique— Correlation with Time

Some dollar figures can be correlated with time passage rather than with another type of activity. Sales is one possible example of this. Perhaps the company has experienced recent growth and has reason to believe that this trend will continue in approximately the same pattern. In situations like this, a least squares regression line can be calculated that shows time passage as the x variable.

It is important to note that the straight line calculated by this method assumes no future significant changes in company policy, economic conditions or other key variables. If such changes are anticipated, the straight-line equation should either be modified or the budgeting technique changed.

The calculation technique is similar to the one explained in the previous section of the chapter. The account that is used

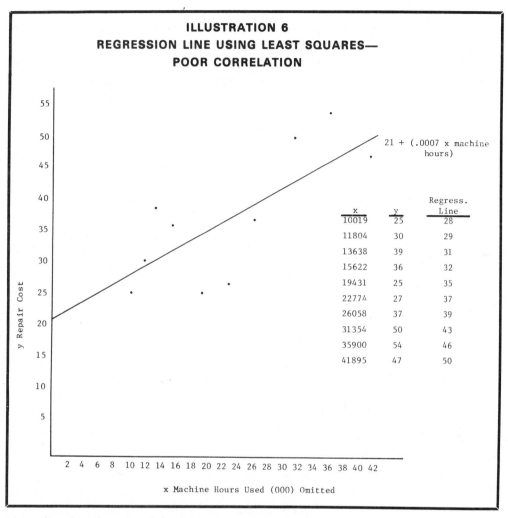

ILLUSTRATION 6
REGRESSION LINE USING LEAST SQUARES—
POOR CORRELATION

21 + (.0007 x machine hours)

x	y	Regress. Line
10019	25	28
11804	30	29
13638	39	31
15622	36	32
19431	25	35
22774	27	37
26058	37	39
31354	50	43
35900	54	46
41895	47	50

y Repair Cost

x Machine Hours Used (000) Omitted

here is sales since it might be time dependent. The following steps are appropriate.

STEP 1. LIST THE SALES AND APPROPRIATE TIME PERIODS.

The criterion for determining time periods is essentially the same here as it was in the previous section. The accountant should avoid selecting too many periods; otherwise, the average trend that is calculated will lose much of its significance.

STEP 2. SQUARE EACH TIME PERIOD. MULTIPLY EACH PERIOD TIMES THE SALES ASSOCIATED WITH THAT PERIOD. CALCULATE THE ARITHMETIC MEAN OF BOTH THE PERIODS AND THE SALES FIGURES. LIST ALL OF THESE AMOUNTS.

Illustration 7 shows the results of steps 1 and 2.

ILLUSTRATION 7
INFORMATION FOR THE CALCULATION
OF A REGRESSION LINE USING
THE LEAST SQUARES METHOD—
CORRELATION WITH TIME

Period x	Total Sales y	x^2	xy
0	$ 10,019	0	$ 0
1	11,904	1	11,904
2	13,638	4	27,276
3	15,622	9	46,866
4	19,431	16	77,724
5	22,774	25	113,870
6	26,058	36	156,348
7	31,354	49	219,478
8	35,900	64	287,200
9	41,895	81	377,055
45	$228,595	285	$1,317,721
Means	$\bar{x} = 4.5$ $\bar{y} = 22,860$		

The two standard formulas used here are:

1. The fixed amount = (the mean of the sales) minus (the mean of the time periods times the variable amount);
2. The variable amount = [(the sum of the individual periods times sales) minus (the mean of the periods times the sum of the sales)] divided by [(the sum of the individual periods squared) minus (the mean of the periods times the sum of the periods)].

The mathematical notations for the formulas are:

1. $a = \overline{y} - b\overline{x}$

2. $b = \dfrac{\Sigma xy - \overline{x}\,\Sigma y}{\Sigma x^2 - \overline{x}\,\Sigma x}$

After substituting numbers from Illustration 7, the formulas read:

1. $a = \$22{,}860 - b\,(4.5)$

2. $b = \dfrac{\$1{,}317{,}721 - (4.5)\,(\$228{,}595)}{285 - (4.5)\,(45)}$

STEP 3. SOLVE THE (b) FORMULA. SUBSTITUTE THE VALUE OF (b) IN THE (a) FORMULA. SOLVE THE (a) FORMULA.

$b = \dfrac{\$289{,}043.50}{\$82.50}$

$b = \$3{,}504$

$a = \$22{,}860 - (\$3{,}504)\,(4.5)$

$a = \$7{,}092$

Using this formula, the regression line shown in Illustration 8 would be calculated for periods 0 through 9. The same illustration shows projections through period 14.

It should be pointed out that the projection of sales into periods 10 through 14 assumes no radical changes in the immediate future. If such changes were anticipated, the above projections would have to be modified. For example, if the accountant, through discussions with sales personnel, has reason to believe that customer coverage will increase, the projections could be increased, i.e., from $3,504 per period to $4,000 per period. On the other hand, an anticipated downward turn in economic activity might decrease the projections, i.e., from $3,504 per period to $3,000 per period.

Illustration 9 shows in chart form the same information as in Illustration 8.

ILLUSTRATION 8
APPLICATION OF REGRESSION LINE
USING THE LEAST SQUARES METHOD—
CORRELATION WITH TIME

Period	Actual Total Sales	Estimated Sales (Regression Line)	Difference
0	$10,019	$ 7,092 *	$2,927
1	11,904	10,596 *	1,308
2	13,638	14,100 *	(462)
3	15,622	17,604 *	(1,982)
4	19,431	21,108 *	(1,677)
5	22,774	24,612 *	(1,838)
6	26,058	28,116 *	(2,058)
7	31,354	31,620 *	(266)
8	35,900	35,124 *	776
9	41,895	38,628 *	3,267
10		42,132 *	
11		45,636 *	
12		49,140 *	
13		52,644 *	
14		56,148 *	
	$228,595		$ (5)

*$7,092 + $3,504 (number of years)

Summary

The key point in evaluating the usefulness of the least squares method is linearity. If recent revenue and expense patterns have been fairly smooth, and if these patterns are expected to continue in the future, this statistical technique will furnish good budget projections. As has been demonstrated, the budget deviations will tend to be minimized. This will save the company personnel valuable time, since it will not be necessary to search out the reason for variations. Illustrations 10-12 are flowcharts of the chapter steps showing how to derive the two regression lines and the coefficient of determination.

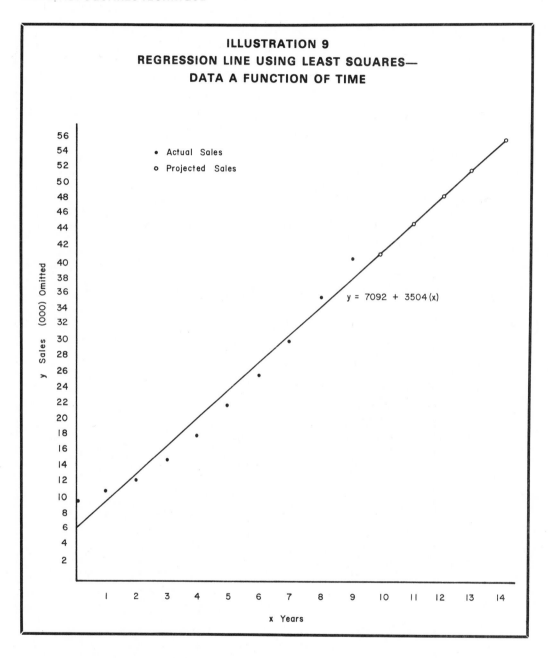

ILLUSTRATION 9
REGRESSION LINE USING LEAST SQUARES—
DATA A FUNCTION OF TIME

• Actual Sales
○ Projected Sales

y = 7092 + 3504 (x)

y Sales (OOO) Omitted

x Years

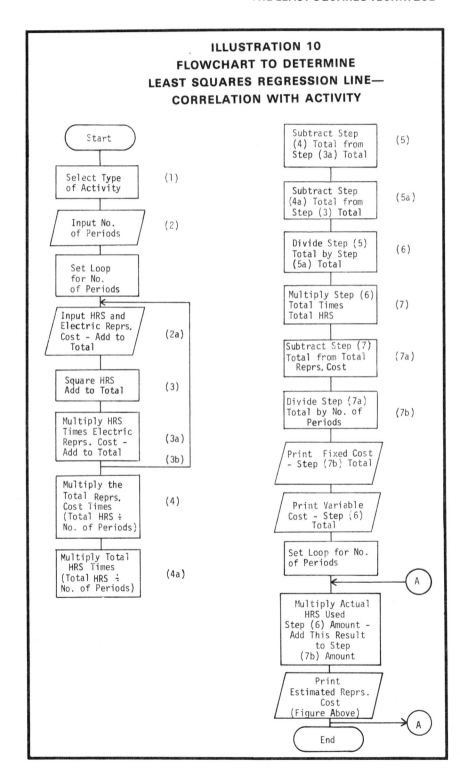

ILLUSTRATION 10
FLOWCHART TO DETERMINE
LEAST SQUARES REGRESSION LINE—
CORRELATION WITH ACTIVITY

Start

Select Type of Activity (1)

Input No. of Periods (2)

Set Loop for No. of Periods

Input HRS and Electric Reprs. Cost - Add to Total (2a)

Square HRS Add to Total (3)

Multiply HRS Times Electric Reprs. Cost - Add to Total (3a) (3b)

Multiply the Total Reprs. Cost Times (Total HRS ÷ No. of Periods) (4)

Multiply Total HRS Times (Total HRS ÷ No. of Periods) (4a)

Subtract Step (4) Total from Step (3a) Total (5)

Subtract Step (4a) Total from Step (3) Total (5a)

Divide Step (5) Total by Step (5a) Total (6)

Multiply Step (6) Total Times Total HRS (7)

Subtract Step (7) Total from Total Reprs. Cost (7a)

Divide Step (7a) Total by No. of Periods (7b)

Print Fixed Cost - Step (7b) Total

Print Variable Cost - Step (6) Total

Set Loop for No. of Periods

A

Multiply Actual HRS Used Step (6) Amount - Add This Result to Step (7b) Amount

Print Estimated Reprs. Cost (Figure Above)

A

End

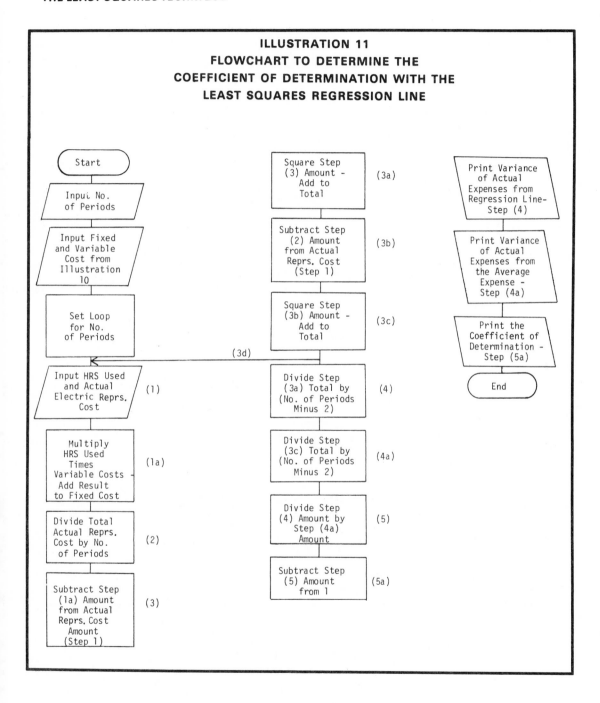

ILLUSTRATION 11
FLOWCHART TO DETERMINE THE
COEFFICIENT OF DETERMINATION WITH THE
LEAST SQUARES REGRESSION LINE

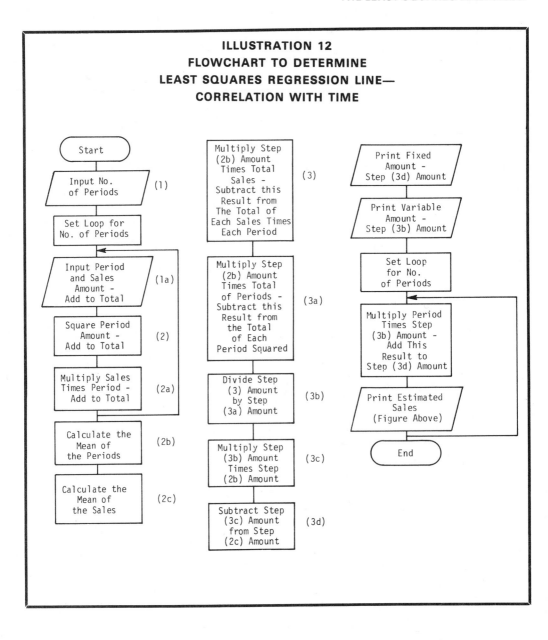

ILLUSTRATION 12
FLOWCHART TO DETERMINE
LEAST SQUARES REGRESSION LINE—
CORRELATION WITH TIME

Start

Input No. of Periods (1)

Set Loop for No. of Periods

Input Period and Sales Amount - Add to Total (1a)

Square Period Amount - Add to Total (2)

Multiply Sales Times Period - Add to Total (2a)

Calculate the Mean of the Periods (2b)

Calculate the Mean of the Sales (2c)

Multiply Step (2b) Amount Times Total Sales - Subtract this Result from The Total of Each Sales Times Each Period (3)

Multiply Step (2b) Amount Times Total of Periods - Subtract this Result from the Total of Each Period Squared (3a)

Divide Step (3) Amount by Step (3a) Amount (3b)

Multiply Step (3b) Amount Times Step (2b) Amount (3c)

Subtract Step (3c) Amount from Step (2c) Amount (3d)

Print Fixed Amount - Step (3d) Amount

Print Variable Amount - Step (3b) Amount

Set Loop for No. of Periods

Multiply Period Times Step (3b) Amount - Add This Result to Step (3d) Amount

Print Estimated Sales (Figure Above)

End

5

The Use of Exponential Smoothing to Forecast Revenues and Costs

In chapter 4, a statistical method was illustrated that assumed future linearity for revenues and costs. In many instances, however, this assumption cannot be made. Although it is true that many costs (direct materials, for example) have short-run linear patterns, there are others that do not.

On the revenue side, sales are often subject to cyclical fluctuations and are sometimes unpredictable. For this and other reasons, recent sales figures may be more meaningful than older ones. The least squares method places proportionate weight on all the prior period amounts that are used in the calculation of the straight line. The technique illustrated here places more emphasis on the *recent* amounts.

Introduction

Exponential smoothing is a mathematical technique that can be used for short-term forecasting. Sales, costs, and prices are examples. Business firms also use this tool in the areas of inventory control and production scheduling. The technique, itself, is a form of a weighted moving average. However, unlike that method, exponential smoothing weights all the previous observations at a declining rate.

Simply, the use of exponential smoothing may be described as follows: If one wishes to forecast sales for the coming period and wishes to use the last ten periods' sales figures as a basis for this forecast, the most recent sales amount will have the most effect on the forecast. The next most recent sales amount will have the second largest effect, etc. By following this pattern, the user is placing the same weights on the prior years' sales that he would probably do intuitively.

Though exponential smoothing is a powerful mathematical tool, it is easy to apply and affords considerable flexibility. By using different smoothing elements (as explained in the next

A Brief Explanation of Exponential Smoothing

section) forecasts can be stabilized or allowed to fluctuate. In addition, exponential smoothing can be simulated conveniently on the computer (as shown in the last chapter).

Although this forecasting technique has many uses, the illustrations in this chapter are confined to techniques that will produce a forecast for one future period of time.

General Methodology

In exponential smoothing, the weights are assigned according to the following method.

Period	Weight if Alpha = .2	Weight if Alpha = .5	Weight if Alpha = .8
Most Recent	.2	.5	.8
All Other Periods	.8	.5	.2

Alpha is a smoothing constant between 0 and 1. A lower alpha value (.2) results in more smoothing and is an appropriate value if it is believed that the previous data upon which the forecast will be designed contain considerable random variations. A higher alpha value (.8) results in less smoothing and is an appropriate value if it is believed that the previous data contain significant variations.

The formula is:

Next period's estimate = (most recent period's actual figure $\times$ alpha) $\times$ [most recent period's estimate of the figure $\times$ (1 − alpha)]

The result of the application of this formula is that the most recent period's observation receives a weight larger than any other. The next most recent period receives the next highest weight, etc.

For example, if actual sales in this period were $1,000 and the prior estimate of this period's sales were $900, next period's estimate would be calculated as follows (assuming the constant, alpha, is .2): $1,000 x .2 = $200

$$900 \times .8 = \underline{\quad 720}$$
$$\underline{\underline{\$920}}$$

On the other hand, if the constant, alpha, is .8, the arithmetic is as follows:

$$\$1{,}000 \times .8 = \$800$$
$$900 \times .2 = \underline{180}$$
$$\underline{\underline{\$980}}$$

Note that the use of a larger alpha percentage is an admission that all the prior figures, other than the most recent, have little meaning. Only the most current sales are indications of future trends. In other words, the future is likely to be rather sporadic and unpredictable.

In Illustration 1 an alpha value of .2 is used. In Illustration 3 a value of .8 is employed. In each case a comparison is made between the results obtained using exponential smoothing and the results obtained using least squares. A flowchart follows the illustrations.

The Application of the Exponential Smoothing Technique

STEP 1.   LIST THE SALES AND THE NUMBER OF TIME PERIODS. FIGURES IN COLUMNS (1) and (2), ILLUSTRATION 1.

STEP 2.   SELECT AN INITIAL SALES ESTIMATE FOR PERIOD 1. AMOUNT IS THE TOP FIGURE IN COLUMN (3), ILLUSTRATION 1.

STEP 3.   MULTIPLY THE LAST PERIOD'S ACTUAL SALES, COLUMN (2), TIMES THE ALPHA CONSTANT. THE RESULT IS IN COLUMN (5).

STEP 4.   MULTIPLY THE LAST PERIOD'S ESTIMATE OF THE SALES, COLUMN (3), TIMES ONE MINUS THE ALPHA CONSTANT. THE RESULT IS IN COLUMN (6). ADD THE TWO ELEMENTS TOGETHER. THE RESULTING FIGURE, COLUMN (3), IS NEXT PERIOD'S ESTIMATE.

ILLUSTRATION 1
EXPONENTIAL SMOOTHING
USING A CONSTANT OF .2

(1)	(2)	(3)	(4)	(5)	(6)
		Estimated		Last Period's Actual	Last Period's Estimated
	Actual	Sales	Difference	Sales Times	Sales Times
Period	Sales	(5) + (6)	(2) − (3)	.2	.8
Initial Estimate	$ —	$ 9,800	$ —	$ —	$ —
1	10,019	9,800	—	—	—
2	11,904	9,844	2,060	2,004	7,840
3	11,000	10,256	744	2,381	7,875
4	10,055	10,405	(350)	2,200	8,205
5	14,212	10,335	3,877	2,011	8,324
6	16,015	11,110	4,905	2,842	8,268
7	12,904	12,091	813	3,203	8,888
8	14,000	12,254	1,746	2,581	9,673
9	15,200	12,603	2,597	2,800	9,803
10	15,100	13,122	1,978	3,040	10,082
11	—	13,518	—	3,020	10,498

ILLUSTRATION 2
LEAST SQUARES USING
DATA FROM ILLUSTRATION 1

Actual Sales	Estimated Sales *	Difference
$10,019	$11,042	$(1,023)
11,904	11,613	291
11,000	12,184	(1,184)
10,055	12,755	(2,700)
14,212	13,326	886
16,015	13,897	2,118
12,904	14,468	(1,564)
14,000	15,039	(1,039)
15,200	15,610	(410)
15,100	16,181	(1,081)
—	16,752	—

*$10,471 + $571 (number of years)

As can be seen from Illustration 1, the estimate of sales gradually increases from period to period despite the fact that the actual sales figures leap back and forth. Note, also, that the differences are fairly large. In this particular set of data, .2 may provide too much of a smoothing influence.

Illustration 2 shows the least squares method applied to the same data.

It is obvious from examining Illustrations 1 and 2 that the least squares technique fits these particular data better than exponential smoothing with an alpha constant of .2.

For purposes of predicting sales patterns, the use of .8 is clearly the best of the three alternatives. (See Illustration 3.) Note that very little smoothing exists in the Estimated column. Although some lag is apparent, the estimated sales tend to drop when actual sales drop, and vice versa.

ILLUSTRATION 3
EXPONENTIAL SMOOTHING
USING A CONSTANT OF .8

(1) Period	(2) Actual Sales	(3) Estimated Sales (5) + (6)	(4) Difference (2) − (3)	(5) Last Period's Actual Sales Times .8	(6) Last Period's Estimated Sales Times .2
Initial Estimate	$ —	$ 9,800	$ —	$ —	$ —
1	10,019	9,800	—	—	—
2	11,904	9,975	1,929	8,015	1,960
3	11,000	11,518	(518)	9,523	1,995
4	10,055	11,104	(1,049)	8,800	2,304
5	14,212	10,265	3,947	8,044	2,221
6	16,015	13,423	2,592	11,370	2,053
7	12,904	15,497	(2,593)	12,812	2,685
8	14,000	13,422	578	10,323	3,099
9	15,200	13,884	1,316	11,200	2,684
10	15,100	14,937	163	12,160	2,777
11	—	15,067	—	12,080	2,987

Illustration 4 contains a summary of the estimations shown in Illustrations 1-3.

	ILLUSTRATION 4			
	SUMMARY OF ESTIMATES			
	IN ILLUSTRATIONS 1-3			
(1)	(2)	(3)	(4)	(5)
			Estimate	
	Actual	Estimate	Using	Estimate
Period	Sales	Using .2	Least Squares	Using .8
1	$10,019	$ 9,800	$11,042	$ 9,800
2	11,904	9,844	11,613	9,975
3	11,000	10,256	12,184	11,518
4	10,055	10,405	12,755	11,104
5	14,212	10,335	13,326	10,265
6	16,015	11,110	13,897	13,423
7	12,904	12,091	14,468	15,497
8	14,000	12,254	15,039	13,422
9	15,200	12,603	15,610	13,884
10	15,100	13,122	16,181	14,937
11	—	13,518	16,752	15,067

Appraisal of the Comparative Results of Exponential Smoothing and Least Squares

It is necessary to understand the major benefit gained from using exponential smoothing. It is a *short-run* predictive device for amounts that are expected to have a sporadic random or nonlinear pattern in the future. The question then becomes one of deciding which method provides the best estimate of sales in the very near future. The accountant should use the $15,067 at the bottom of the right-hand column in Illustration 4. This is the estimate using an alpha of .8. It is the figure most responsive to the sporadic nature of the recent period's actual sales.

Illustration 5 is a chart that shows how the three estimates in Illustration 4 fit the actual sales data. Several things should be noted about the comparative trend lines.

1. The least squares line is linear. However, it is of no practical use to the accountant because of the lack of correlation between the actual sales and the time periods.

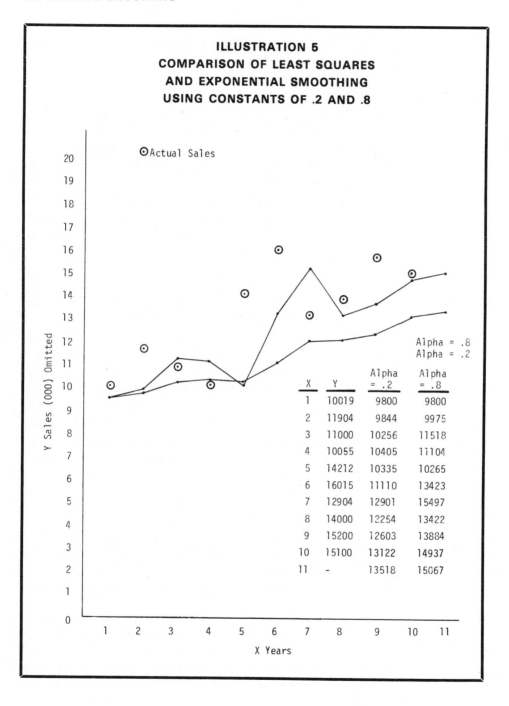

ILLUSTRATION 5
COMPARISON OF LEAST SQUARES
AND EXPONENTIAL SMOOTHING
USING CONSTANTS OF .2 AND .8

⊙Actual Sales

Y Sales (000) Omitted

Alpha = .8
Alpha = .2

X	Y	Alpha = .2	Alpha = .8
1	10019	9800	9800
2	11904	9844	9975
3	11000	10256	11518
4	10055	10405	11104
5	14212	10335	10265
6	16015	11110	13423
7	12904	12901	15497
8	14000	12254	13422
9	15200	12603	13884
10	15100	13122	14937
11	–	13518	15067

X Years

2. The exponential smoothing line with an alpha constant of .2 is almost linear and therefore suffers from the same drawback as the least squares line. If the data are slightly nonlinear, exponential smoothing with a .2 factor might provide a better projection than least squares.
3. Exponential smoothing with an alpha constant of .8 shows the greatest amount of curve in the trend line. It is probably the best projection technique for these particular data. Given the history of sales for the last ten periods, there is little reason to believe that a constant period increase of $571 will occur. The .8 trend line provides projections to match the sporadic history and the anticipated sporadic future.

Summary

The use of exponential smoothing requires that a certain amount of experimentation be done. Different values of alpha should be fitted to historical data until a reasonably good fit emerges. It is possible that the anticipated future pattern is totally unpredictable. In such a case, some other budget method must be employed. It is unlikely, however, that most accounts will have this characteristic. It is quite probable that certain revenues or costs (unit or dollar sales, for example) have future patterns that are dependent, in part, on recent past revenues or costs. If accountants are aware of this situation, they can provide management with some helpful quantitative aids.

Exponential smoothing as it is shown here is not a particularly good method for projecting amounts beyond one period. The reason for this is apparent when the various illustrations are examined. It is necessary to have the current period's actual amount in order to calculate next period's estimate.

It is also apparent that there is a considerable amount of similarity between the use of low alpha values and least squares. The advantage of low alpha values is that they provide a curved trend to project historical data that are essentially nonlinear.

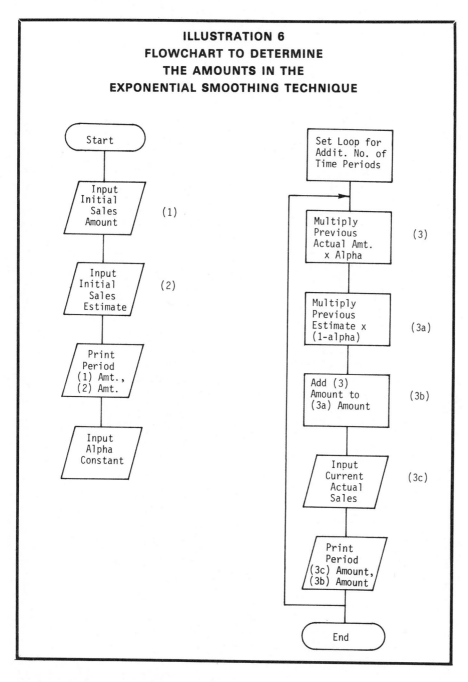

ILLUSTRATION 6
FLOWCHART TO DETERMINE
THE AMOUNTS IN THE
EXPONENTIAL SMOOTHING TECHNIQUE

Illustration 6 is a flowchart explanation of the exponential
smoothing technique steps.

6

The Use of
Linear Programming in the
Deployment of Resources
to Different Segment Lines

The accountant's reporting function has expanded far beyond the historical Balance Sheet and Income Statement. He is now expected to provide management with a wide variety of financial analyses. One of the most popular reports that is furnished by the accountant is Income Statement data by company segments. The segment can be (1) product lines, (2) territories, (3) divisions, (4) departments, or perhaps some combination of several of these.

The Accountant's Contribution to Management Information

ILLUSTRATION 1
THE OLDER AND MORE TRADITIONAL
METHOD OF PRESENTING INCOME
STATEMENT DATA BY SEGMENTS

	Total	Division A	Division B	Division C
Sales or Revenue	$100,000	$30,000	$40,000	$30,000
Cost of Sales				
Materials Used	30,000	10,000	8,000	12,000
Direct Labor	12,000	6,000	3,000	3,000
Overhead Applied	15,000	7,000	5,000	3,000
	$ 57,000	$23,000	$16,000	$18,000
Gross Profit	$ 43,000	$ 7,000	$24,000	$12,000
Operating Expenses				
Salaries	25,000	8,000	10,000	7,000
Advertising	6,000	1,800	2,400	1,800
Other	8,000	2,400	3,200	2,400
	$ 39,000	$12,200	$15,600	$11,200
Net Income	$ 4,000	$ (5,200)	$ 8,400	$ 800

The sharp focus that is now being placed on fixed and variable costs has added a new dimension to segment reporting. Illustrations 1 and 2 show the difference between the more traditional method and the newer techniques for deciding how to employ dollar resources where the most profit per dollar of expenditure will result.

ILLUSTRATION 2
THE NEWER METHOD OF
PRESENTING INCOME STATEMENT
DATA BY SEGMENTS

	Total	Division A	Division B	Division C
Sales or Revenue	$100,000	$30,000	$40,000	$30,000
Variable Expenses				
Materials Used	30,000	10,000	8,000	12,000
Direct Labor	12,000	6,000	3,000	3,000
Variable Overhead	6,000	3,000	1,500	1,500
Delivery Expense	3,000	1,500	700	800
Other	3,000	700	1,000	1,300
	$ 54,000	$21,200	$14,200	$18,600
Contribution Margin	$ 46,000	$ 8,800	$25,800	$11,400
Fixed Expenses				
Fixed Overhead	9,000	4,000	3,500	1,500
Salaries	25,000	8,000	10,000	7,000
Advertising	6,000	1,800	2,400	1,800
Other	2,000	200	1,500	300
	$ 42,000	$14,000	$17,400	$10,600
Net Income	$ 4,000	$ (5,200)	$ 8,400	$ 800

The Contribution Margin and Deployment of R & D Funds

Assume that the company has research funds available to employ among the various divisions. Assume that the use of these funds would normally be expected to increase unit sales. The data in Illustration 2 are of *some* help because they show contribution margin. Illustration 3 shows how.

ILLUSTRATION 3
CONTRIBUTION MARGIN ANALYSIS
OF THE DATA IN ILLUSTRATION 2

	Division A	Division B	Division C
Sales	$30,000	$40,000	$30,000
Contribution Margin	8,800	25,800	11,400
Contribution Margin % (Rounded)	29	63	38

It appears that Division B has a big edge in requesting research funds. In the short run, every dollar of sales in Division B is expected to increase contribution margin and net income by approximately $.63. For Division A and Division C, the expectations are $.29 and $.38, respectively.

It is possible, however, that it might take different amounts of research dollars to produce extra sales in each division. If the accountant learns that this is true, the analysis shown in Illustration 4 is appropriate.

ILLUSTRATION 4
RESEARCH FUNDS PRODUCE VARYING
SALES INCREASES IN EACH DIVISION

	Division A	Division B	Division C
Contribution Margin % — from Illustration 3	29	63	38
Amount of Extra Sales That Could Be Generated by a Dollar of Research Applied to That Division	$5.00	$2.00	$1.00
Contribution Margin Per Dollar of Research Expended (Extra Sales Times %)	$1.45	$1.26	$ .38

In this case it is obvious that Division A is in a slightly better position to ask for the research dollar.

The Use of Contribution Margin Analysis to Allocate Advertising Funds for Greater Profit Return

A similar analysis can be made on the use of advertising money. If it is possible to project a probable ratio between a dollar of advertising expenditure and the incremental sales of a company segment, a quantitative example similar to Illustration 4 can be helpful.

The segment line may be classified by products in addition to or in place of divisions, departments, or territories. In this case, production time might be the critical input. Accountants can furnish aid to their company or client by making up a segment line statement similar to the one shown in Illustration 5.

ILLUSTRATION 5
PRODUCTION TIME PRODUCES VARYING
UNIT INCREASES FOR EACH PRODUCT LINE

	Product A	Product B	Product C
Sales Per Unit	$5.00	$3.00	$2.00
Variable Expenses Per Unit	3.00	1.50	1.20
Contribution Margin Per Unit	$2.00	$1.50	$ .80
Amount of Units That Can Be Made with an Hour of Productive Time	1	2	3
Contribution Margin Per Hour	$2.00	$3.00	$2.40

The situation here is similar to the case in Illustration 4. Product B seems to have the edge because it will produce the highest contribution margin per productive hour.

The Use of Linear Programming

The reader can observe that each succeeding illustration contains a more sophisticated approach to segment line decision:

1. Illustration 1 contains very little information to help the firm make necessary segment line decisions.

2. Illustration 2 introduces the *dollar* amount of contribution margin.
3. Illustration 3 carries the analysis a step further and calculates contribution margin percentages.
4. Illustrations 4 and 5 introduce the concept of contribution margin per dollar or per hour of scarce input factor.

This section of the chapter contains analyses that make use of linear programming techniques to decide which segments should receive all or any portion of the input factor (research dollar, advertising dollar, productive hours, etc.).

Linear programming is a technique that can be employed when several characteristics of a business problem exist.

A Concise Definition of Linear Programming

1. There is a need to optimize some desirable feature; i.e., maximize some type of profit figure or minimize a cost. In this case, the accountant is concerned with maximizing the total contribution margin of all the segments.
2. The numerical relationships are assumed to be linear. For example, the contribution margins per unit in Illustration 5 are $2.00, $1.50 and $.80, respectively. This is a 1, .75, .40 relationship. In linear programming calculations, these relationships are expected to remain intact.
3. There are one or more constraints due to scarce resources, maximum capacity, etc.

Although the accountant may employ a number of procedures to solve linear programming situations, the more direct and practical method is to test all the feasible combinations until one is found that provides a better solution than any other feasible combination. This is the manner in which the solutions in this chapter are derived.

Assume that the company has three territories in which it operates. Television, radio and newspaper advertising is used in all three areas. Each territorial advertising expenditure is separate and distinct. The best evidence that is available to market researchers shows that a dollar of advertising would normally be expected to produce the following:

A Description of the Accountant's Model Situation

$3.00 of Sales and a 40 percent Contribution Margin for Territory 1.

$3.50 of Sales and a 30 percent Contribution Margin for Territory 2.

$3.50 of Sales and a 40 percent Contribution Margin for Territory 3.

The budget situation compels the firm to limit the advertising cost to $20,000. In addition, there is a practical limitation to the amount of advertising that can be placed in the news media of all three territories. The limitation is $10,000, $15,000 and $8,000 in Territories 1, 2 and 3, respectively.

The situation described above can be expressed as shown in Illustration 6.

ILLUSTRATION 6
EXPRESSION OF ADVERTISING ALLOCATION SITUATION IN EQUATION FORM

Dollar Contribution Margin per Dollar of Advertising for Territory 1 ($3.00 $\times$ 40% = $1.20)

Dollar Contribution Margin per Dollar of Advertising for Territory 2 ($3.50 $\times$ 30% = $1.05)

Dollar Contribution Margin per Dollar of Advertising for Territory 3 ($3.50 $\times$ 40% = $1.40)

X_1 = Proper Amount of Advertising to Territory 1
X_2 = Proper Amount of Advertising to Territory 2
X_3 = Proper Amount of Advertising to Territory 3
M = Maximized Total Contribution Margin
TA = Total Advertising Funds that can be Spent ($20,000)
A_1 = Total Advertising That Can Be Spent in Territory 1 ($10,000)
A_2 = Total Advertising That Can Be Spent in Territory 2 ($15,000)
A_3 = Total Advertising That Can Be Spent in Territory 3 ($8,000)

Equation (1) $M = \$1.20 \, X_1 + \$1.50 \, X_2 + \$1.40 \, X_3$
Equation (2) $TA \leq \$20,000$
Equation (3) $A_1 \leq \$10,000$
Equation (4) $A_2 \leq \$15,000$
Equation (5) $A_3 \leq \$ 8,000$

The $20,000 of advertising is to be apportioned in such a way as to maximize total contribution margin.

STEP 1. CALCULATE THE CONTRIBUTION MARGIN PER DOLLAR OF ADVERTISING FOR EACH SEGMENT.

Allocation of Advertising Money in Order to Maximize Total Contribution Margin

The amounts in Illustration 6 are $1.20, $1.05 and $1.40 for Territories 1, 2, and 3, respectively.

STEP 2. DETERMINE THE MAXIMUM AMOUNT OF ADVERTISING MONEY THAT CAN BE EXPENDED.

The amount in this example is $20,000.

STEP 3. DETERMINE THE MAXIMUM AMOUNT OF ADVERTISING MONEY THAT CAN BE SPENT IN EACH OF THE SEGMENTS.

From Illustration 6 the figures of $10,000, $15,000 and $8,000 are used for Territories 1, 2, and 3, respectively.

STEP 4. DETERMINE AN INITIAL FEASIBLE SOLUTION. CALCULATE THE TOTAL CONTRIBUTION MARGIN IF THE ADVERTISING DOLLARS ARE APPORTIONED IN THIS MANNER.

The accountant may start at any point desired. A convenient place is the allocation of money to Territory 1, up to its maximum of $10,000. The rest of the money goes to Territory 2, up to its maximum or up to the maximum amount left. The rest, if any, goes to Territory 3, up to its maximum. The result of this allocation is shown below.

	Territory 1	Territory 2	Territory 3	Total
Advertising Dollars	$10,000	$10,000	0	
Times Contribution Margin Per Advertising Dollar	1.20	1.05	1.40	
Contribution Margin	12,000	10,500	0	$22,500

STEP 5. **MOVE FROM THE INITIAL FEASIBLE SOLUTION IN STEP 4 TO ANOTHER FEASIBLE SOLUTION. CONTINUE CALCULATING THE TOTAL CONTRIBUTION MARGIN THAT WILL BE PRODUCED BY EVERY FEASIBLE SOLUTION.**

STEP 6. **ALLOCATE THE ADVERTISING DOLLARS TO EACH SEGMENT USING THE COMBINATION IN STEP 5 THAT PRODUCES THE LARGEST TOTAL CONTRIBUTION MARGIN.**

Illustration 7 shows all the feasible combinations and the contribution margin associated with each possibility. The maximum contribution margin can be earned by allocating $10,000, $2,000 and $8,000 to Territories 1, 2 and 3, respectively. A final test of this solution can be made by assuming the following:

Territory 3 with the largest contribution margin per dollar of expenditure receives all of the advertising money up to its maximum of $8,000.

Territory 1 with the next largest contribution margin per dollar of expenditure receives the next amount of advertising money up to its maximum of $10,000.

Territory 2 with the smallest contribution margin per dollar of expenditure receives the rest of the advertising money up to its maximum of $15,000, if any money is left.

ILLUSTRATION 7
FEASIBLE COMBINATIONS OF ALLOCATION
OF ADVERTISING DOLLARS TO SEGMENTS—
DATA TAKEN FROM ILLUSTRATION 6

Description of Territory Allocation	Territory 1	Territory 2	Territory 3	Total Contribution Margin
1 first, 2 next, 3 next	$10,000 × $1.20 = $12,000	$10,000 × $1.05 = $10,500	$ 0 × $1.40 = $ 0	$22,500
1 first, 3 next, 2 next	$10,000 × $1.20 = $12,000	$ 2,000 × $1.05 = $ 2,100	$8,000 × $1.40 = $11,200	$25,300
2 first, 1 next, 3 next	$ 5,000 × $1.20 = $ 6,000	$15,000 × $1.05 = $15,750	$ 0 × $1.40 = $ 0	$21,750
2 first, 3 next, 1 next	$ 0 × $1.20 = $ 0	$15,000 × $1.05 = $15,750	$5,000 × $1.40 = $ 7,000	$22,750
3 first, 1 next, 2 next	$10,000 × $1.20 = $12,000	$ 2,000 × $1.05 = $ 2,100	$8,000 × $1.40 = $11,200	$25,300
3 first, 2 next, 1 next	$ 0 × $1.20 = $ 0	$12,000 × $1.05 = $12,600	$8,000 × $1.40 = $11,200	$23,800

Comments on the Method

The accountant who uses the techniques explained in this chapter can expect to maximize profits. If the company used the information in Illustration 1 as a guideline in allocating advertising funds, most of the money would go to Division B since its net income is considerably higher than the other two. It is possible that no advertising funds would go to Division A. If *no* quantitative techniques were employed, an "intuitive" division of the expenditures would probably result in a lower total contribution margin.

For example, assume that management, without the benefit of the quantitative tools explained in this chapter, arbitrarily assigns one-third of the $20,000 advertising budget to each territory. Illustration 8 shows the lost contribution margin that would result from this decision.

ILLUSTRATION 8
LOST CONTRIBUTION MARGIN FROM
ASSIGNING ONE-THIRD OF THE $20,000
ADVERTISING BUDGET TO EACH TERRITORY—
DATA FROM ILLUSTRATIONS 6 AND 7

Description of Territory Allocation	Territory 1	Territory 2	Territory 3	Total Contribution Margin
One-Third to Each	$6,666 x $1.20 = $8,000	$6,666 x $1.05 = $7,000	$6,666 x $1.40 = $9,333	$24,333
Maximum Contribution Margin in Illustration 7				25,300
Lost Contribution Margin				$ 967

Reference to Illustrations 6, 7 and 8 shows that in each of the company segments the anticipated contribution margin per dollar of advertising expenditure is greater than $1.00. What if studies revealed that a dollar of advertising could be expected to yield less than a dollar of contribution margin in any segment? In that case, it is unlikely that any of the budget would be spent in this area, unless there were other reasons to do so. This, of course, makes the accountant's contribution even more important.

Illustration 9 contains a flowchart diagramming the steps previously explained.

Flowchart to Demonstrate Previous Steps

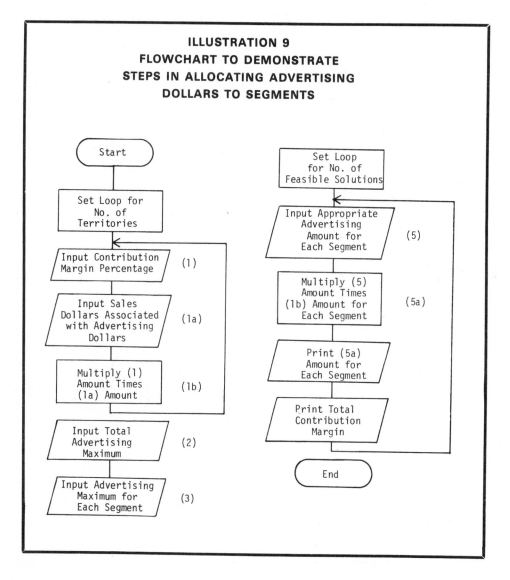

**ILLUSTRATION 9
FLOWCHART TO DEMONSTRATE
STEPS IN ALLOCATING ADVERTISING
DOLLARS TO SEGMENTS**

Use of Product Line Segments to Enhance Production Line Profits

The accountant can aid the company's profit position by rendering reports on the amount of production time that should be devoted to different products, given certain types of constraints. This particular technique is applicable to decisions regarding two segments.

Assume that the contribution margin per hour of production time is $2.00 and $3.00 for products A and B, respectively. Assume that the maximum number of units per month that can be produced by A and B is 150 and 200. Furthermore, the maximum monthly production time that can be generated on the two segment lines is 160 hours. The accountant's problem is to decide how many hours (and thus how many units) should be allocated to each product.

This situation is similar to the one posed in the earlier section of the chapter. There are some differences, however. Illustration 10 contains a list of the equations.

ILLUSTRATION 10
EXPRESSION OF PRODUCTION PROBLEM
SITUATION IN EQUATION FORM

(1) Maximized Total Contribution Margin
(M) = (Contribution Margin Per Unit of Product A x No. Units) + (Contribution Margin Per Unit of Product B x No. Units)

or

M = $2.00 A + $1.50 B

(2) One hour of production time creates one unit of A and one hour of production time creates two units of B. The total hourly capacity is 160. Therefore, one unit per hour of A + two units per hour of B ≤ 160 total hours,

or

One A + Two B ≤ 160

(3) A's unit capacity is 150. B's unit capacity is 200. Therefore:
A ≤ 150
B ≤ 200

Although it is not necessary, the accountant can facilitate the solving of this problem by drawing a graph similar to the one shown in Illustration 11.

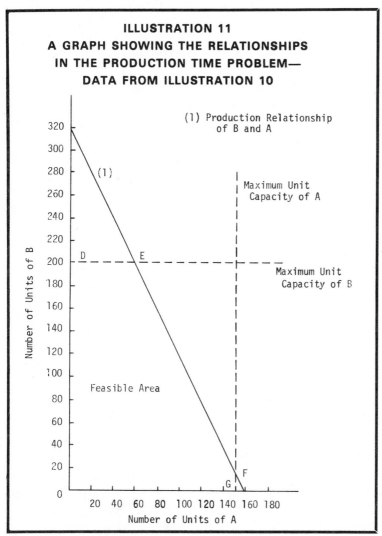

ILLUSTRATION 11
A GRAPH SHOWING THE RELATIONSHIPS
IN THE PRODUCTION TIME PROBLEM—
DATA FROM ILLUSTRATION 10

(1) Production Relationship of B and A

Maximum Unit Capacity of A

Maximum Unit Capacity of B

Feasible Area

Number of Units of B

Number of Units of A

Several items should be noted about this graph that will help the accountant communicate its meaning to other members of the management team.

1. The vertical axis represents the number of units of B. The top horizontal line extending from 200 units of B means

that this is the practical unit capacity of B. If this limita-
tion did not exist, 320 units of B could be made with the
maximum hourly capacity of 160.

2. The horizontal axis represents the number of units of A.
The vertical line extending upward from 150 means that
this is the practical unit capacity of A. This constraint also
has meaning since it dominates the 160 unit constraint due
to the hourly capacity of 160. In other words, 160 units of
A could be produced with 160 capacity hours if it were not
for the fact that A has a maximum unit capacity of 150.

3. The line extending from 320 units of B down to 160 units
of A expresses a basic relationship between the two
products. Twice as many units of B can be produced with
the same number of hours.

4. The feasible production area is bounded by C, D, E, F and
G. The feasible production areas are points C, D, E, F and
G.

Illustration 12 shows how the accountant can move through
all possible solutions. The methodology is essentially the
same as the advertising problem previously described. The
point C feasible solution of no production is ignored.

Contribution margin is maximized when 60 hours of production time is devoted to product A and 100 hours is used for
product B. This is option (2) and point E on the graph in
Illustration 11.

Comments on the Use of This Method

Reference to Illustration 5 shows that the contribution
margin per unit is $2.00 for product A and only $1.50 for
product B. If this comparison were used as the only basis for
allocating the scarce time resource, the firm would have
chosen to give product A all of the productive time it could
take (150 hours) with the rest going to B. Thus, option (3) in
Illustration 12 probably would have been chosen and the
result would have been $90 in lost profit.

On the other hand, the *lower* portion of Illustration 5
provides comparative figures that are more meaningful for
this type of problem. The contribution margin per *hour* of

ILLUSTRATION 12
FEASIBLE COMBINATIONS OF THE ALLOCATION OF PRODUCTION TIME TO SEGMENTS—
DATA TAKEN FROM ILLUSTRATION 11

Point On Illustration 11 Graph	Product A				Product B				Total
	Hours	Units	Contribution Margin Per Unit	Contribution Margin	Hours	Units	Contribution Margin Per Unit	Contribution Margin	
D	0	0	$2.00	$ 0	100	200	$1.50	$300	$300 (1)
E	60	60	2.00	120	100	200	1.50	300	420 (2)
F	150	150	2.00	300	10	20	1.50	30	330 (3)
G	150	150	2.00	300	0	0	1.50	0	300 (4)

production time is $2.00 for product A and $3.00 for product B. The reader can refer to option (2) in Illustration 12 and see that this alternative involves granting to product B its maximum number of hours (100) with the rest going to A. This type of comparison cannot always be made because of the complexity of the variables. However, it does demonstrate that the accountant must often look beyond contribution margin per *unit* in his analysis.

Summary and Critique

The techniques explained in this chapter merely add a new quantitative element to contribution margin analysis. It is a valuable tool that can be employed by the accountant to help the firm maximize short-run profits. Other analyses (both quantitative and nonquantitative) will undoubtedly be made. The solutions suggested here, however, will provide a valuable addition to the list.

7

Sampling Unnumbered Documents by Use of a Computer-Generated Random Number Table

More and more accountants are making practical use of statistical sampling techniques to effectively interpret ever-growing amounts of data in business. External auditors use these techniques to shorten the sample size and to provide them with a more scientific basis for evaluating client records. Industrial and government accountants have also learned the value of statistical sampling and apply it to such things as inventory and census counts. A problem arises, however, in trying to assign random numbers to a population or set of un-numbered items—such as cash receipt transactions or physical inventory—to facilitate systematic sampling.

One solution is to label the items or documents. When this is not feasible (and often it is not), another possibility is to draw random numbers from a table and to arrange these numbers by hand is ascending sequential order. The sampling is then done by intervals, similar to the systematic method. The advantage is that the numbers are selected according to simple random sampling methods. The disadvantage is that the procedure is time consuming when the sample size is large.

The increasing use of real-time computer terminals, however, has opened up new possibilities. Computer programs that generate random numbers are available (or can be written). By combining a sort routine with a random number generator, the samples can be arranged in ascending sequential order. The program can then be stored on disk or some other secondary storage device and called into core memory whenever desired. With a different initialing, the program will generate a unique set of random numbers. The maximum size of the number table generated by each computer run is determined by the limitations of the individual computer system.

The set of 50 numbers in Illustration 1 is an example of a table that can be generated by a random number formula. The items are arranged in sequential order.

ILLUSTRATION 1				
A TABLE OF 50 RANDOM NUMBERS				
ARRANGED IN ASCENDING SEQUENTIAL ORDER				
016	525	956	1343	1525
070	546	1039	1358	1533
095	657	1054	1359	1662
107	731	1060	1374	1693
134	767	1066	1403	1770
146	768	1178	1446	1821
184	832	1264	1473	1861
264	835	1266	1507	1870
438	873	1304	1512	1966
495	918	1308	1513	1983

There are at least three different ways in which a table of this type can be used:

1. The documents or items are prenumbered and the population size is known. The figures above can then represent the document or item numbers. This is the most simple and direct way to use a table of random numbers.
2. The documents or items are *not* prenumbered but the population size is known. In this case the numbers in the table can be thought of as intervals, e.g., the 16th, 70th item, etc.
3. The documents or items are not prenumbered *and* the population size is *not* known. As long as the necessary sample size and the number of digits in the population are known, a table can be constructed that will be appropriate. Assume that the accountant needs a sample of 100 out of a population that does not exceed 3 digits (no larger than 999). A random number table can be created like the one in Illustration 2.

**ILLUSTRATION 2
A TABLE OF 100 RANDOM NUMBERS
ARRANGED IN ASCENDING SEQUENTIAL
ORDER—ASSUMING A POPULATION OF 3 DIGITS**

030	232	373	551	749
033	234	386	552	760
034	237	394	558	762
052	240	399	568	771
060	252	399	577	781
063	257	407	596	794
066	279	425	597	795
084	282	430	600	807
087	293	435	606	811
124	304	449	649	848
146	314	455	652	853
147	315	491	659	867
167	317	494	660	881
174	320	495	661	882
180	325	500	662	890
190	353	507	675	932
214	354	508	677	934
215	355	512	684	962
226	366	515	700	971
228	371	533	729	976

STEP 1: DECIDE HOW MANY DIGITS ARE IN THE POPULATION. CREATE A RANDOM NUMBER TABLE THAT HAS THE PRESCRIBED NUMBER OF DIGITS AND THE PRESCRIBED NUMBER OF SAMPLES.

Steps to Take if the Population Is Not Known

Reference to Illustration 2 shows that the desired sample size is 100 and that there are 3 digits in the population.

STEP 2: PERFORM INTERVAL SAMPLING ON THE UN-NUMBERED DOCUMENTS OR ITEMS UNTIL THE POPULATION TOTAL HAS BEEN REACHED. THEN START OVER AT THE BEGINNING OF THE POPULATION.

Assume that the population total is 800. Reference to Illustration 2 reveals that the highest sample number below 800 is 795. Yet 795 is only the 87th number in the table. If 100 is the desirable sample size, then 13 more numbers must be selected. It is obvious that no number above 800 can be used since 800 is the population total. The answer to the dilemma is to start all over at the beginning of the population. Item 807 in the table becomes number 7 in the population; item 811 in the table becomes number 11 in the population, etc. Finally, item 976 in the table becomes number 176 in the population.

Other Considerations

It is possible that the accountant has underestimated the number of digits in the population. For example, the population used in Illustration 2 might have been 1030 rather than 800; 976 is the last number in the table and 976 is also the last sample. This means, of course, that the last 30 items in the population have no chance of being selected unless the sample size is enlarged.

There are three ways to overcome this problem:

1. The accountant can ignore the remaining elements in the population. If the population size is 1030 and the table only allowed for 999 (3 digits), some small portion of the population has no chance of being sampled. Although this is a practical solution, it is theoretically wrong to exclude any part of the population from possible sample selection. If the population size is well over 1000, a difficult problem has been created and this alternative should not be followed.
2. The accountant can increase the size of his sample. There is no need to generate another table if the population size is 1030. A printed table of random numbers can be used and the small number of additional samples can be selected and arranged in sequential order by hand. An additional table should be generated if the population size is significantly larger than 999.
3. The problem can be anticipated and a 4-digit table can be

created. This appears to be the best alternative, unless the anticipated sample size is barely over 3 digits (1030).

Illustration 4 contains random numbers generated by a 4-digit table.

ILLUSTRATION 4 A TABLE OF 100 RANDOM NUMBERS ARRANGED IN ASCENDING SEQUENTIAL ORDER—ASSUMING A POPULATION OF 4 DIGITS				
0309	2323	3736	5510	7497
0332	2349	3866	5523	7605
0340	2371	3948	5583	7621
0520	2408	3991	5687	7712
0600	2524	3997	5770	7817
0634	2577	4072	5964	7941
0668	2797	4255	5979	7953
0849	2858	4306	6007	8073
0871	2935	4356	6064	8112
1234	3047	4490	6495	8487
1466	3145	4555	6529	8531
1478	3153	4917	6591	8670
1675	3177	4943	6603	8818
1745	3203	4951	6607	8820
1802	3257	5003	6627	8900
1906	3539	5077	6752	9324
2144	3540	5085	6772	9341
2156	3559	5124	6845	9622
2266	3660	5152	7003	9716
2289	3718	5333	7298	9760

The same procedure can be followed here. When the end of the population is reached, the accountant should start all over. For example, if the population total is 6000, the next sample after 5979 is item or document number 7 in the population (6007). The last sample is item or document number 3760 (9760).

**Making the
Table of
Random Numbers
Correspond to the
Population Total**

If the accountant can make a close estimate of the population total, the random number tables become even more useful. Assume, for example, that a sample size of 50 is needed. In addition to knowing the number of digits in the population, the accountant also has a *general* idea of what the population total might be. This estimate of the total is 2000. A table can be generated that produces a sample of 50 out of a population of 2000. Such a table is shown in Illustration 5.

ILLUSTRATION 5				
A TABLE OF 50 RANDOM NUMBERS				
ARRANGED IN ASCENDING SEQUENTIAL				
ORDER—ASSUMING A POPULATION OF 2000				
0016	0525	0956	1343	1525
0070	0546	1039	1358	1533
0095	0657	1054	1359	1662
0107	0731	1060	1374	1693
0134	0767	1066	1403	1770
0146	0768	1178	1446	1821
0184	0832	1264	1473	1861
0264	0835	1266	1507	1870
0438	0873	1304	1512	1966
0495	0918	1308	1513	1983

If the actual population total is only 1900 (2000 being a close estimate), the accountant can treat 1966 in the table as 66 in the population; 1983 in the table can also be treated as 83 in the population; 66 and 83 can easily be arranged into the array.

**Summary
Comments**

Even without benefit of the computer, the accountant can arrange random numbers in ascending sequential order. When unnumbered documents or items are being sampled, this is a time-saving procedure. When computers are available, still more time is saved. The convenience of systematic sampling (every 10th item, every 20th item, etc.) is retained and the basis for the sample is more scientifically sound.

As the population becomes larger, the problem of numbering the items or documents becomes even more acute. The arranging of random numbers in sequential order (either by hand or with a computer program) can save the external and internal accountant several hours of valuable time.

8

The Combined Use
of Variable and
Attribute Sampling

Attribute sampling has long been a useful device to auditors in testing internal control in independent audits. This sampling method can also be used on tests of the year-end inventory and accounts receivable. Sometimes these amounts are verified by means of interim work. For example, accounts receivable confirmation requests can be sent out in October and the results tabulated at that time. If the auditors can establish the fairness of the October figure, they will assume (with the aid of additional tests) that the December year-end figure is fair.

The audit of accounts receivable lends itself very well to attribute sampling, but after the probable error rate has been estimated, there may still be a question as to whether the *dollar* amount of the errors is significant. For example, the auditors may find only four errors in a sample of 100, but the dollar size of these errors may cause the auditors to wonder whether the accounts receivable figure is materially misstated. One way to provide evidence on this question is to sample for variables as well as for attributes. The following is an example of such a combined test.

Assume the auditor has a client with 1000 customers and that the accounts receivable (book amount) is $1,490,000. The auditor decides to use combined attribute and variable sampling. The methodology is as follows.

STEP 1: USING STANDARD ATTRIBUTE SAMPLING TECHNIQUES, DETERMINE THE NUMBER OF ACCOUNTS THAT NEED TO BE CONFIRMED.

In order to do this, the auditors must decide the highest error rate in the population that they will tolerate (upper precision

*In the chapter Appendix, there is an explanation of attribute sampling.

limit). Assume that this rate is 9% (or a maximum of 90 errors out of 1000 accounts).* They must make an estimate of the actual error rate that exists in the population. Based on prior experience and/or judgment, this percentage is determined to be about 4%. Thus, 100 accounts are confirmed. (See Table 2 in the Appendix.)

STEP 2: MAKE A TALLY OF THE CONFIRMATION RESULTS.

This tally should include not only the *number* of errors but the amount of each error and an indication as to whether the error represents an understatement or an overstatement in the client's reported balance. This tally is shown in Illustration 1.

STEP 3: DECIDE WHETHER THE NUMBER OF ERRORS FALLS WITHIN THE ACCEPTABLE RANGE.

If the sample results show an upper limit precision percentage that is too high, then the test results are unsatisfactory. However, assume that four errors are found out of a sample of 100. Reference to Table 3 in the Appendix indicates that this gives an upper limit precision percentage of 8.92% at a reliability of 95%. Thus, the attribute sampling is considered to be successful.

STEP 4: MAKE A DOLLAR TALLY OF THE CONFIRMATION RESULTS.

Illustration 1 shows this tally.

---

*This rate may appear to be high, but rates such as this are suggested in auditing publications for "noncritical tests."

ILLUSTRATION 1
A TALLY OF CONFIRMATION RESULTS*
(Some of the tally of 100 accounts is omitted)

(1) Client Book Amount	(2) Audit Confirmation Amount	(3) Difference	(4) Book Amount Squared	(5) Differences Squared	(6) Book Amount x Difference
$ 1,363	$ 1,363	$ –	$ 1,857,769	$ –	$ –
1,903	703	(1,200)	3,621,409	1,440,000	(2,283,600)
1,929	959	(970)	3,721,041	940,900	(1,871,130)
1,723	1,723	–	2,968,729	–	–
1,092	1,092	–	1,192,464	–	–
1,566	1,046	(520)	2,452,356	270,400	(814,320)
1,127	1,127	–	1,270,129	–	–
1,566	126	(1,440)	2,452,356	2,073,600	(2,255,040)
1,898	1,898	–	3,602,404	–	–
—	—	(OMITTED ACCOUNTS)	—	—	—
$142,500	$138,370	$(4,130)	$231,875,040	$4,724,900	$7,224,090

*If the auditor has reason to believe that the sample differences are not typical of the population differences, he should make a further check of the client's records. Otherwise the results may be misleading.

127

STEP 5: CALCULATE THE STANDARD DEVIATION OF THE POPULATION OF RATIOS IN THE SAMPLE OF 100 IN ILLUSTRATION 1. REFER TO THE ILLUSTRATION TOTALS.

(a) Divide the column (3) total ($4,130) by the sum of the sample client book amounts, the column (1) total ($142,500).
Answer: (.029)

(b) Square the answer in (a).
Answer: (.000841)

(c) Double the answer in (a).
Answer: (.058)

(d) Multiply the column (4) total (231,875,040) x (b) (.00084).
Answer: $195,007

(e) Multiply (c) (.058) x the column (6) total ($7,224,090).
Answer: $418,997

(f) Add the column (5) total ($4,724,900) to (d) ($195,007).
Answer: ($4,919,907)

(g) Subtract (e) from (f).
Answer: $4,919,907 − $418,997 = $4,500,910

(h) Divide (g) ($4,500,910) by the sample size minus 1 (99).
Answer: $45,464

(i) Take the square root of (h). This is the standard deviation of the sample of ratios and is the best estimate of the standard deviation of the population of ratios.
Answer: 213 (rounded off)

STEP 6: CALCULATE THE PRECISION.

(a) Multiply the answer in Step 5(i) (213) x the reliability coefficient (1.96) x population size (1000).
Answer: $417,480

(b) Divide (a) by the square root of the sample size (100).
Answer: $417,480 ÷ 10 = $41,748

(c) Multiply (b) by an adjustment factor. This factor is the square root of [1 — (the sample size 100÷ the population size 1000)].
Answer: $39,661

STEP 7: MAKE AN ESTIMATE OF THE POPULATION TOTAL.

Multiply .971 (1 − .029) x the client's book amount ($1,490,000).

Answer: $1,446,790

STEP 8: DETERMINE, AT THE APPROPRIATE CONFIDENCE LEVEL (95%), THE PRECISION RANGE AROUND THE POPULATION ESTIMATE.

$1,446,790 + $39,661 = $1,486,451
$1,446,790 − $39,661 = $1,407,129

The book population total is $1,490,000; therefore, the results of the variable sampling are not acceptable since the book total is higher than the upper precision range.

Summary

If the reader obtains unsatisfactory results with the attribute sampling, take whatever steps are desirable to adjust for acceptable compliance with internal control. If satisfactory results are obtained with attribute sampling but inspection of the dollar amount of errors indicates a potential problem, apply this special variable sampling technique (ratio estimation). If the book amount is not within the precision range at the specified confidence level, further investigation is recommended.

Appendix to Chapter 8
Explanation of Attribute Sampling

General Discussion

Attribute sampling is a method of determining the range within which the percentage of errors in the population falls, as contrasted with variable sampling which is a method of determining the range within which the dollar amount of the population falls. Each error is treated as one item regardless of its magnitude. This type of sampling is used for testing of transactions, such as tests of extensions, authorizations or postings.

Attribute sampling normally requires less time than variable sampling since tables are available that indicate the necessary sample size to achieve the desired results. Three percentages should be known or estimated:

1. The auditors need to know the highest error rate that is tolerable. For example, a test examination of postings from the sales journal to the accounts receivable ledger will undoubtedly uncover some errors. Without needing to know the population total, the auditor can set 4% (an example) as the highest tolerable error rate. If the sample results show, at a certain degree of reliability, that the error percentage does not exceed 4%, then the auditor is satisfied that *this* part of the client's system is reliable enough.
2. The auditor must decide on the degree of reliability that is acceptable, e.g., 90% certainty that the client's representation is within the desired precision limits.
3. The auditors need an estimate of the actual error rate in the population. In the absence of any prior experience with the records, the auditor can take a preliminary sample and base his estimate on the result of this sample. For example, if a preliminary sample of 50 produces two errors, the best estimate of the population error rate is 4%.

The percentage used in point 3, above, is not necessarily the same percentage that is used in point 1. While the auditor may think that the actual error rate is 4%, there may be a willingness to accept a 90% probability (reliability) that the highest error in the population is 6% (upper limit of precision).

Auditors do not confine the use of attribute sampling to tests of transactions. This method is also used in accounts receivable confirmation and other areas in which errors may be found by comparing figures. In general, attribute sampling is less time consuming than variable sampling and is probably more popular with professional and industrial accountants.

Table 1 is used to determine the sample size. Assume that the estimated occurrence rate is 4%, (1) in the table. Assume that the upper limit precision is 8.9, (2) in the table. The table itself is a 95% reliability table. The sample size is 100, (3) in the table.

Table 2 is used to evaluate the sample results. Assume a sample of 100. Reference the 100 samples and size bloc, (1) in the table. Reference the number of errors, (2) in the table. Reference the reliability column, (3) in the table. The attained precision is 8.92, (4) in the table.

The Use of Attribute Sampling Tables

TABLE 1
DETERMINATION OF SAMPLE SIZE—TABULAR FORM
ONE-SIDED UPPER PRECISION LIMITS
Reliability Level—95.0 Percent

SAMPLE SIZE	OCCURRENCE RATE									
	0.0	.5	1.0	2.0	3.0	4.0[1]	5.0	6.0	7.0	8.0
50	5.8			9.1		12.1		14.8		17.4
100[3]	3.0		4.7	6.2	7.6	8.9[2]	10.2	11.5	13.0	14.0
150	2.0			5.1		7.7		10.2		12.6
200	1.5	2.4	3.1	4.5	5.8	7.1	8.3	9.5	10.8	11.9
250	1.2			4.2		6.7		9.1		11.4
300	1.0		2.6	3.9	5.2	6.4	7.6	8.8	10.0	11.1
350	.9			3.7		6.2		8.5		10.8
400	.7	1.6	2.3	3.6	4.8	6.0	7.2	8.3	9.5	10.6
450	.7			3.5		5.9		8.2		10.4
500	.6		2.1	3.4	4.6	5.8	6.9	8.0	9.2	10.3
550	.5			3.3		5.7		7.9		10.1
600	.5	1.3	2.0	3.2	4.4	5.6	6.7	7.8	9.0	10.0
650	.5			3.2		5.5		7.7		10.0
700	.4		1.9	3.1	4.3	5.4	6.6	7.7	8.8	9.9
750	.4			3.1		5.4		7.6		9.8
800	.4	1.1	1.8	3.0	4.2	5.3	6.4	7.5	8.7	9.7
850	.4			3.0		5.3		7.5		9.6
900	.3		1.7	3.0	4.1	5.2	6.3	7.5	8.5	9.5
950	.3			2.9		5.2		7.4		9.4
1000	.3	1.0	1.7	2.9	4.0	5.2	6.3	7.4	8.4	9.4
1500	.2		1.5	2.7	3.8	4.9	5.9	6.9	7.9	8.9
2000	.1	.8	1.4	2.6	3.7	4.7	5.7	6.7	7.7	8.7
2500	.1		1.4	2.6	3.6	4.6	5.6	6.6	7.6	8.6
3000	.1	.8	1.4	2.5	3.5	4.5	5.5	6.5	7.5	8.5
4000	.1	.7	1.3	2.4	3.4	4.4	5.4	6.4	7.4	8.4
5000	.1	.7	1.3	2.3	3.3	4.3	5.3	6.3	7.3	8.3

9.0	10.0	12.0	14.0	16.0	18.0	20.0	25.0	30.0	40.0	50.0
	19.9	22.3	25.1	27.0	29.6	31.6		42.4	52.6	62.4
15.4	16.4	18.7	21.2	23.3	25.6	27.7	33.1	38.4	48.7	56.6
	15.0	17.3	19.6	21.7	24.0	26.1		36.7	47.0	56.8
13.1	14.2	16.4	18.7	20.9	23.1	25.2	30.5	35.7	45.7	55.6
	13.7	15.9	18.1	20.3	22.4	24.6		34.8	44.8	54.7
12.2	13.3	15.5	17.7	19.8	22.0	24.1	29.1	34.1	44.1	54.1
	13.0	15.2	17.4	19.5	21.7	23.6		33.6	43.6	53.6
11.7	12.8	15.0	17.2	19.2	21.2	23.2	28.2	33.2	43.2	53.2
	12.6	14.8	16.8	18.9	20.9	22.9		32.9	42.9	52.9
11.4	12.5	14.6	16.7	18.6	20.7	22.6	27.6	32.6	42.6	52.6
	12.3	14.4	16.4	18.4	20.4	22.4		32.4	42.4	52.4
11.2	12.2	14.2	16.2	18.2	20.2	22.2	27.2	32.2	42.2	52.2
	12.1	14.1	16.1	18.1	20.1	22.1		32.1	42.1	52.1
10.8	11.9	13.9	15.9	17.9	19.9	21.9	26.9	31.9	41.9	51.9
	11.8	13.8	15.8	17.8	19.8	21.8		31.8	41.8	51.8
10.7	11.7	13.7	15.7	17.7	19.7	21.7	26.7	31.7	41.7	51.7
	11.6	13.6	15.6	17.6	19.6	21.6		31.6	41.6	51.6
10.5	11.5	13.5	15.5	17.5	19.5	21.5	26.5	31.5	41.5	51.5
	11.4	13.4	15.5	17.4	19.5	21.4		31.5	41.5	51.5
10.4	11.4	13.4	15.4	17.4	19.4	21.4	26.4	31.4	41.4	51.4
9.9	10.9	12.9	14.9	16.9	18.9	20.9	25.9	30.9	40.9	50.9
9.7	10.7	12.7	14.7	16.7	18.7	20.7	25.7	30.7	40.7	50.7
9.6	10.6	12.6	14.6	16.6	18.6	20.6	25.6	30.6	40.6	50.6
9.5	10.5	12.5	14.5	16.5	18.5	20.5	25.5	30.5	40.5	50.5
9.4	10.4	12.4	14.4	16.4	18.4	20.4	25.4	30.4	40.4	50.4
9.3	10.3	12.3	14.3	16.3	18.3	20.3	25.3	30.3	40.3	50.3

TABLE 2
EVALUATION OF SAMPLE RESULTS

		UPL* RELIABILITY LEVEL	
Number of Occurrences	90%	95%(3)	99%
SAMPLE SIZE 25			
0	8.80	11.29	16.82
1	14.69	17.61	23.75
2	19.91	23.10	29.59
3	24.80	28.17	34.88
4	29.47	32.96	39.79
SAMPLE SIZE 50			
0	4.50	5.82	8.80
1	7.56	9.14	12.55
2	10.30	12.06	15.77
3	12.88	14.78	18.72
4	15.35	17.38	21.50
5	17.76	19.88	24.15
6	20.11	22.32	26.71
8	24.69	27.02	31.61

		UPL* RELIABILITY LEVEL	
Number of Occurrences	90%	95%	99%
SAMPLE SIZE 75			
0	3.02	3.92	5.96
1	5.09	6.17	8.53
2	6.94	8.16	10.74
3	8.69	10.01	12.78
4	10.38	11.79	14.70
5	12.02	13.51	16.55
6	13.62	15.18	18.34
7	15.20	16.82	20.08
8	16.75	18.42	21.77
12	22.78	24.63	28.25
SAMPLE SIZE 100(1)			
0	2.28	2.95	4.50
1	3.83	4.66	6.45
2	5.23	6.16	8.14
3	6.56	7.57	9.70
4(2)	7.83	8.92(4)	11.17
5	9.08	10.23	12.58
6	10.29	11.50	13.95
7	11.49	12.75	15.29
8	12.67	13.97	16.59
9	13.83	15.18	17.87
10	14.99	16.37	19.13
11	16.13	17.55	20.37
15	20.61	22.15	25.18

*Upper Precision Limit

SAMPLE SIZE 150

Number of Occurrences	UPL* RELIABILITY LEVEL		
	90%	95%	99%
0	1.52	1.98	3.02
1	2.57	3.12	4.34
2	3.51	4.14	5.49
3	4.40	5.09	6.54
4	5.26	6.00	7.54
5	6.10	6.88	8.50
6	6.92	7.74	9.44
7	7.72	8.59	10.35
8	8.52	9.42	11.24
9	9.31	10.24	12.12
10	10.09	11.05	12.98
11	10.86	11.85	13.83
12	11.62	12.64	14.67
13	12.39	13.43	15.50
14	13.14	14.21	16.32
15	13.89	14.98	17.13
16	14.64	15.75	17.94
23	19.79	21.02	23.42

SAMPLE SIZE 125

Number of Occurrences	UPL* RELIABILITY LEVEL		
	90%	95%	99%
0	1.83	2.37	3.62
1	3.08	3.74	5.19
2	4.20	4.95	6.55
3	5.27	6.09	7.81
4	6.29	7.17	9.00
5	7.29	8.23	10.15
6	8.27	9.25	11.26
7	9.24	10.26	12.34
8	10.19	11.25	13.40
9	11.13	12.23	14.44
10	12.06	13.19	15.47
11	12.98	14.15	16.48
12	13.89	15.09	17.47
13	14.80	16.03	18.45
19	20.14	21.50	24.16

*Upper Precision Limit

135

9

The Use of a Quantitative Internal Control Questionnaire to Help Determine Reliability Percentage in Sampling

In addition to its traditional uses, statistical sampling allows accountants to make definite statements about the degree of certainty concerning their conclusions. This degree of certainty is expressed as a reliability or confidence level percentage and generally takes this form:

> There is 95 percent confidence that the correct population total is within ± $10,000 of our estimate of the figure.

If some form of attribute sampling is being conducted, the statement might be worded in this manner:

> There is 95 percent confidence that the error rate in the population is ± 2 percent of our estimate of the error rate.

It is important that consideration be given to the size of the reliability percentage since a higher figure results in a larger sample size. Extracting and evaluating additional samples could take hours of effort. If this added effort is performed by the external auditor, it will add to the total audit fee. If internal auditors carry out this additional sampling, a diversion of company resources will result.

Current Use of Statistical Sampling by Accountants

In the past, little attention was given to the derivation of this important quantitative element. The auditor's judgment was considered to be sufficient. In recent years, however, there have been suggestions in accounting publications that reliability should be a partial function of internal control. The American Institute of Certified Public Accountants has stated that the evaluation of internal control should be a major factor in determining reliability.

Reliability and Internal Control

This chapter contains a description of a *specific* method that may be employed to give the user of internal control questionnaires a quantitative guide in establishing a reliability or confidence level percentage. There is no suggestion here that these *particular* weights should be attached to the questionnaire. This is simply a model that can be applied to any phase of an external or internal audit. If it results in a lower required reliability and a lower sample size, time and money can be saved.

ILLUSTRATION 1
PARTIAL DESCRIPTION OF THE
SALES AND ACCOUNTS RECEIVABLE SYSTEM

Each department has one cash register through which all charge and cash sales in that department are carried. Customers who pay cash are given a register slip while those who charge merchandise are asked to sign a sales ticket. One copy of this ticket is given to the customer immediately, and the other two copies are filed away in the register drawer.

Each morning a member of the Controller's staff "clears" all the registers of the media associated with cash sales, charge sales and sales returns. These media are taken to the Controller's department where various reports are made out including the daily sales report. One copy of the charge sales ticket and the sales return ticket is used to make out the daily sales report and the other copy is given to the accounts receivable clerk for posting.

Collections on account are handled both by mail and over the counter. In each case the receipts are turned over to the cashier and the slips that accompany the receipts are given to the Controller's staff for inclusion in the daily cash report. The daily cash report includes both collections on account and cash sales. The receipt slips are then turned over to the accounts receivable clerk for posting.

For purposes of this explanation, it is assumed that the auditor is circularizing confirmation requests to accounts receivable customers. Among other things, it will be necessary to predetermine the acceptable reliability percentage so that the sample size of confirmations can be calculated. Illustration 1 contains a partial description of the system being employed by the company.

Use of the Internal Control Questionnaire to Determine Reliability

---

The daily sales report serves as a book of original entry. The monthly totals are posted directly to the general ledger as debits to accounts receivable and sales returns and credits to sales and accounts receivable. The daily cash report also serves as a book of original entry with its monthly totals being posted as debits to cash and sales returns, and credits to sales and accounts receivable.

A ledger card is maintained for each customer. The clerks post charges to the accounts from the charge sales tickets that are used to create the daily sales report. Noncash credits are posted from return tickets that constitute a part of the daily report and from other authorized media. Mechanical posting machines are used to perform the billing function.

Customer company uses the cycle billing process that is fairly common in retail department stores. Different parts of the alphabet are billed at "staggered" times throughout the month so that the clerks' workload on the accounts may be eased and more timely and accurate statements issued to the customer. Each mailed statement includes the medium that is used to update the account (sales tickets, return tickets, and receipt tickets).

Journal entries for writing off uncollectable accounts must be authorized on a memo signed by the manager of the credit department. Other journal entries must be approved by the Controller.

Illustration 2 contains some examples of internal control questions. Below each question is an explanation of the importance that an auditor might attach to that particular inquiry. In addition, there is a scale of ten upon which the relative importance can be recorded.

ILLUSTRATION 2
A PARTIAL INTERNAL CONTROL QUESTIONNAIRE
RELATED TO THE SALES AND ACCOUNTS
RECEIVABLE SYSTEM DESCRIBED IN
ILLUSTRATION 1

1. Are prenumbered sales tickets used for charge sales and credits and are these tickets controlled by someone other than sales personnel?

The auditor might consider this control to be reasonably important since it decreases the chances of illegitimate charges flowing through the system. Assume that the auditor records an importance rating of 6, and that the answer is "no."

2. Is someone other than the accounts receivable clerk responsible for making out sales reports from the charge and credit documents?

The auditor is likely to consider this an extremely important control feature for obvious reasons. Failure to separate these duties could result in accounts receivable personnel failing to charge certain accounts. Assume that the auditor records an importance rating of 10 and that the answer to this question is "yes."

3. Are the functions of handling cash and recording the cash credits to customers separated?

This feature, like number 2 above, will probably be considered very critical. If these duties are not separated, lapping could occur. Assume that the auditor records an importance rating of 10 and that the answer to this question is "yes."

4. When collections on account are opened by the mail clerk, is a separate listing made before the receipt slips are released to another party?

While most auditors will agree on the desirability of such a control feature, it is probably not as important as others since the cash and the receipt slips are handled independently. For purposes of this example, a rating of 4 is given and the answer to the question is "no."

5. Is the total of the accounts receivable customer accounts balanced with the general ledger control figure before billings are sent out?

This procedure represents a final check on the accuracy of the charges and credits to the customer accounts before statements are mailed. Despite the built-in controls described above, errors could remain undetected if this routine were not carried out. Assume a rating of 9 and assume that the answer is "yes."

6. Does an internal auditing staff independently send out periodic confirmation requests to customers?

If postings were made to the wrong account, customer replies might reveal this discrepancy. However, internal auditing staffs are not always practical to maintain. Most auditors are not likely to find this procedure as essential as some of the others. Assume a rating of 3 and assume that the answer is "no."

7. Does someone outside the accounts receivable department approve noncash credits to customer accounts?

This control will possibly be considered important because of the possible consequences of not having it. Accounts receivable clerks might credit a friend's account and fake a sales return document. The importance of this feature would probably be diminished if the accounts receivable personnel do not have access to the cash. Therefore, a rating of 8 is assigned. Assume that the answer to this question is "yes."

Most internal control questionnaires undoubtedly will contain more inquiries than the ones listed in Illustration 2. Each question should be weighted according to the same scale. It will also be necessary to translate the weights and the answers into a reliability percentage. Illustration 3 contains a conversion table.

ILLUSTRATION 3
TABLE FOR CONVERTING INTERNAL
CONTROL QUESTIONNAIRE WEIGHTS AND ANSWERS
INTO A RELIABILITY PERCENTAGE

Assume a 95% reliability factor if no consideration is given to internal control.

Assume that .5% will be subtracted from the above factor for every weighted point with a "yes" answer. Also, .5% will be added to the above factor for every weighted point with a "no" answer.

The final reliability percentage is calculated as follows.

Starting Percentage		95.0%
Subtract:		
Question 2—Yes Answer—Weight of 10	5.0%	
Question 3—Yes Answer—Weight of 10	5.0	
Question 5—Yes Answer—Weight of 9	4.5	
Question 7—Yes Answer—Weight of 8	4.0	18.5
		76.5%
Add:		
Question 1—No Answer—Weight of 6	3.0%	
Question 4—No Answer—Weight of 4	2.0	
Question 6—No Answer—Weight of 3	1.5	6.5
Final Reliability Percentage		83.0%

A lower reliability percentage, of course, means a smaller sample size, which, in turn, means time and money are saved on the audit. It does *not* diminish the quality of the work or change the significance of the findings. It merely allows the external and internal auditor the opportunity to make use of good internal control procedures.

If the answers to all the questions in Illustration 4 were "yes," the reliability factor would drop from 83 percent to 70 percent according to the following calculation.

A Change in the Weights and Answers

Subtotal from Illustration 3	76.5%
Subtract Yes Answers to Questions 1, 4, 6	6.5
Final Reliability Percentage	70.0%

Assume that the answers to Questions 5 and 7 were "no." This would mean that the customer accounts are not balanced against the general ledger account and that noncash credits are not independently approved. In this case, the external or internal auditor might consider the overall system to be weak. The revised reliability factor reflects this opinion.

Final Percentage from Illustration 3	83%
Add Question 5 and Question 7 Percentage	
Instead of Subtracting [(4.5% x 2) + (4.0% x 2)]	17%
	100%
Or, More Realistically	99%+

This is simply another way of stating that due to the weakness in this system of internal control, the auditor will have to have an extremely high degree of reliability on substantive or dollar tests. The sample size will need to be enlarged in order to provide this confidence level.

If the auditor feels that certain questions are given too much or too little weight, changes can be made. An example is Question 7. Some auditors may grade this 4 rather than 8. This would result in a 2 percent change rather than a 4 percent change and would change the confidence level requirement to 85 percent. The conversion table in Illustration 3 is quite flexible and provides a unique reliability percentage with each set of assumptions. The user may include any question that is considered relevant. The weights are a matter of individual judgment and, if the reader wishes, he may change the original reliability amounts by more or less than .5 percent.

A Description of the Steps

STEP 1. DECIDE WHICH QUESTIONS ON INTERNAL CONTROL ARE RELEVANT TO THE SUBSEQUENT DOLLAR TESTS.

Any part of the system that directly affects sales or accounts receivable should be included. This is largely a matter of judgment.

STEP 2. DECIDE ON WHAT THE RELIABILITY WOULD BE IF NO RECOGNITION IS MADE OF THE POSSIBLE EFFECT OF INTERNAL CONTROL.

The strength or weakness of the control system is only one determinant of the reliability percentage. A system that is stronger than average should lower the percentage, and vice versa. Ninety-five percent is selected here because of its relative popularity in accounting practice.

STEP 3. ASSIGN WEIGHTS TO EACH RELEVANT QUESTION BASED ON THE AUDITOR'S EVALUATION OF ITS IMPORTANCE.

This routine is also a function of judgment. The auditor will be influenced by the questions that are more critical to (1) the safeguarding of the firm's assets, and (2) the reliability of the firm's records. Questions 2 and 3 seem to fit in this category since they involve duties that obviously should be split. Fraud and/or account misstatement could result if the responsibilities are not separated. However, a weight of 10 is assigned to these two questions for illustrative purposes. The reader may prefer smaller weights.

STEP 4. DETERMINE A "YES" OR "NO" ANSWER TO EACH SELECTED QUESTION.

STEP 5. DECIDE WHAT EFFECT A WEIGHTED "YES" OR "NO" ANSWER WOULD HAVE ON THE ORIGINAL PERCENTAGE IN STEP 2.

The selection of .5 percent for each weighted "yes" or "no" is arbitrary (a "yes" answer on weight of 4 means 2 percent is subtracted). Each user should recognize that a weighted positive response results in a subtraction from the original reliability percentage. Likewise, a negative answer creates an addition to the original percentage.

STEP 6. IF THE ANSWER TO A GIVEN INQUIRY IS "YES," SUBTRACT .5 PERCENT FOR EACH WEIGHT GIVEN TO THAT QUESTION (5 PERCENT FOR A WEIGHT OF 10, ETC.). IF THE ANSWER TO A QUESTION IS "NO," ADD .5 PERCENT FOR EACH WEIGHT GIVEN TO THAT QUESTION.

STEP 7. MAKE A TALLY OF THE FINAL RELIABILITY PERCENTAGE.

Flowchart to Determine Final Reliability Percentage

Illustration 4 contains a flowchart of the procedures described throughout this chapter.

Summary

One of the advantages of the method illustrated in this chapter is the versatility of its use. The reader may decide on the number of questions to enter and he may also choose the type. Different weights may be attached to each question and decisions may be formulated on the appropriate percentage change for each answer. Thus, a large variety of answers can be generated depending on the judgment of the user.

The evaluation of internal control includes more than a questionnaire. Flowcharts, narrative descriptions, and oral inquiries are used. Results from application of these methods could change the auditor's reliability. Also, tests of com-

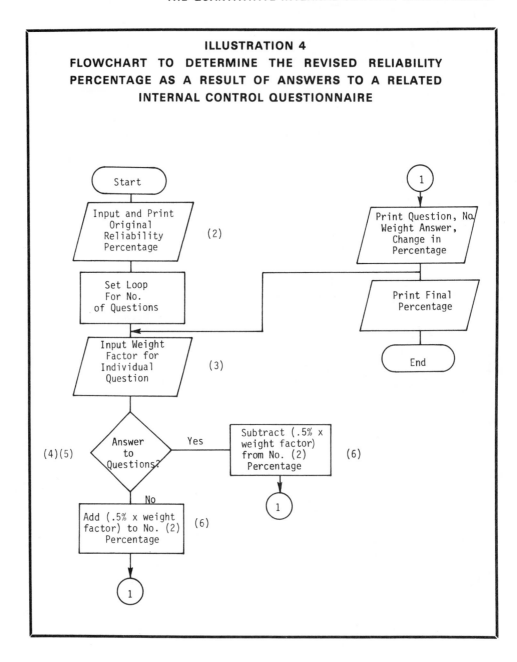

ILLUSTRATION 4
FLOWCHART TO DETERMINE THE REVISED RELIABILITY
PERCENTAGE AS A RESULT OF ANSWERS TO A RELATED
INTERNAL CONTROL QUESTIONNAIRE

pliance must be made in order to assure the auditor that the system in question is actually functioning as it should. These tests include such things as checking proper authorizations, examining signatures and endorsements, etc. These procedures are necessary in order to determine the validity of "yes" and "no" answers on the control questionnaire. For example, the auditor should follow up a "yes" answer to inquiry number 7 in Illustration 2 by actually examining non-cash credit documents to ascertain that the proper authorization signature is on the document. A "yes" answer to Question 7 should not lower the reliability percentage unless this control feature is actually being carried out.

10

FORTRAN
Computer Programs

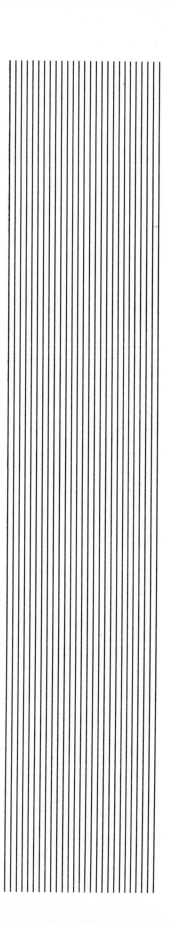

This chapter contains FORTRAN computer programs for some of the statistical and quantitative applications illustrated in chapters 1-9. With EDP systems becoming more commonplace, these programs should provide an opportunity for accountants to use the statistical and quantitative methods that otherwise may appear overly burdensome to manipulate by hand.

The FORTRAN language was chosen because of its widespread use in the business world. In addition, FORTRAN steps can be read and interpreted by noncomputer personnel, especially with the explanations that accompany these steps.

Following each program are examples of (1) hypothetical input, (2) an indication of how the input can be arranged for processing, and (3) the output produced by the hypothetical input. These items, along with the program listings and accompanying explanations, represent a package that can be used immediately if a compatible computer is available. These applications are particularly suitable to IBM terminals.

There are some possible minor alterations that should be mentioned, however. The READ and WRITE statements are written for a particular computer. For example, the statement READ (5,9)C means to read according to FORMAT Statement Number 9 and to read punched card input. The number 5 refers to punched card input. Likewise, WRITE (6,5) means to write according to FORMAT Statement 5 and to write on a printer. The first number inside the parentheses should be changed to correspond to the computer equipment used by the reader's particular company.

Also, the programs for the illustrations in chapters 3 and 6 are written for a certain number of items of input. If a different quantity of input is desired, program modifications should be made (a FORTRAN programmer can do this easily). Finally, the FORMAT (1X .....) statements followed by the WRITE statement just below can be deleted if punched card input is used. These statements are intended for on-line terminal use and a neater printed output shows up if they are omitted for use with punched card input.

The computer programs need not be used intact to afford benefit to the reader. These programs can be modified by data processing personnel (it is much easier to modify a program to a particular use than to write an original program). Then, too, these program listings and explanations should stimulate the desire of accountants to suggest more computer applications in accounting and other financial areas.

FORTRAN PROGRAM TO DETERMINE
EXCESS PRESENT VALUE
FOR CHAPTER 1—ILLUSTRATION 6

	Program Step		Reference to Flowchart Step and/or Explanation
5	FORMAT (1X, 'INPUT THE INVESTMENT COST')		To Print User Instructions
7	WRITE (6,5)		
8	DIMENSION X (100), Y(100), Z(100)		To Reserve Locations for Arrays
9	FORMAT(F7.0)		To Format the Input
10	READ (5,9)C	(1)	To Input Investment Cost
12	FORMAT (1X, 'INPUT NO. OF ESTIMATES')		
14	WRITE (6,12)		To Print User Instructions
18	FORMAT (I2)		To Format the Input
20	READ (5,18)N	(1)	To Input Number of Estimates
21	R2 = 0		To Set Up Grand Total Summing Area
30	DO 246 I = 1,N,1		To Set Loop for Number of Estimates
32	FORMAT (1X, 'INPUT SALVAGE VALUE FOR ESTIMATE', I2)		
34	WRITE (6,32) I		To Print User Instructions
38	FORMAT (F4.0)		To Format the Input
40	READ (5,38)S	(2)	To Input Salvage Value
42	FORMAT (1X, 'INPUT TAX RATE FOR ESTIMATE', I2)		
44	WRITE (6,42)I		To Print User Instructions
48	FORMAT (F2.2)		To Format the Input
50	READ (5,48) T	(3)	To Input Tax Rate

Program Step	Reference to Flowchart Step and/or Explanation
51 P2 = 0	To Set Up Summing Area for Present Value Total
52 FORMAT (1X, 'INPUT NO. YRS. OF LIFE')	To Print User Instructions
53 WRITE (6,52)	To Format the Input
55 FORMAT (I2)	To Input Number of Years of Life
56 READ (5,55)M	To Set Loop for Number of Years of Life
60 DO 170 K = 1,M,1	
62 FORMAT (1X, 'INPUT CASH FLOW FOR YEAR', I2)	To Print User Instructions
64 WRITE (6,62) K	To Input the Format
68 FORMAT (F6.0)	
70 READ (5,68)F	(5) To Input the Cash Flow
80 C1 = C − S	(6) To Subtract Salvage Value from Cost
82 FORMAT (1X, 'INPUT DEPREC. RATE FOR YEAR', I2)	
84 WRITE (6,82)K	To Print User Instructions
88 FORMAT (F3.3)	To Format the Input
90 READ (5,88)R	To Input Depreciation Rate
100 D = C1 *R	(6a) Computations
110 S1 = D *T	(6b) Computations
120 F1 = F *T	(6c) Computations
130 T1 = F1 − S1	(6d) Computations
140 F2 = F − T1	(7) Computations
142 FORMAT (1X, 'INPUT PRESENT VALUE % FOR YEAR' I2)	
144 WRITE (6,142)K	To Print User Instructions
148 FORMAT (F3.3)	To Format the Input
150 READ (5,148)P	To Input Present Value Percentage

```
160   P1 = F2 * P                                                        (8)   Computations
170   P2 = P2 + P1                                                        (8)   Computations
190   AL = S * P                                                         (10)   Computations
200   P3 = AL + P2                                                       (10)   Computations
210   P4 = P3 − C                                                        (10)   Computations
212   FORMAT (1X, 'INPUT PROBABILITY %')                                 (11)   Computations
214   WRITE (6,212)                                                            To Print User Instructions
218   FORMAT (F2.2)                                                            To Format the Input
220   READ (5,218)E                                                            To Input Probability Percentage
230   E1 = P4 * E                                                        (12)   Computations
240   E2 = E2 + E1                                                       (12)   Computations
242   X(I) = P4                                                                To Place Output in Arrays
244   Y(I) = E                                                                 To Place Output in Arrays
246   X(I) = E1                                                                To Place Output in Arrays
247   FORMAT (24X, 'EXCESS P.V.' 24X, 'PROB.',
      24X, 'EXPECTED EXCESS P.V.')                                             To Format the Headings
248   WRITE (6,247)                                                            To Print the Headings
249   DO 260 I = 1,N,1                                                         To Set Loop for Printout of Totals
250   FORMAT (24X, F9.2, 26X, F4.2, 25X, F9.2)
260   WRITE (6,250) X (I), Y(I), Z(I)                                          To Print Totals
270   FORMAT (24X, 'TOTAL EXPECTED EXCESS P.V.',
      39X, F9.2)
290   WRITE (6,270) E2                                                         To Print Grand Total
300   STOP
      END
```

EXAMPLE OF INPUT AND OUTPUT FOR FORTRAN COMPUTER PROGRAM TO DETERMINE EXCESS PRESENT VALUE FOR CHAPTER 1 — ILLUSTRATION 6

INPUT

Description of Variable	Variable Name Used in Program	5-Year Life		6-Year Life		7-Year Life	
		Amount	Columns on Card or Other Type of Input	Amount	Columns on Card or Other Type of Input	Amount	Columns on Card or Other Type of Input
Cost	C	0010000	1-7	001000	1-6	000900	1-6
Number of Estimates	N	03	1-2				
Salvage Value	S	002000	1-6				
Tax Percentage	T	50	1-2	50	1-2	50	1-2
Number of Years of Life	M	05	1-2	06	1-2	07	1-2
Cash Flow	F	002600	1-6	002600	1-6	002600	1-6
Depreciation Percentage	R	200	1-3	167	1-3	143	1-3
Present Value Percentage	P	909	1-3	909	1-3	909	1-3
Cash Flow	F	002600	1-6	002600	1-6	002600	1-6
Depreciation Percentage	R	200	1-3	167	1-3	143	1-3
Present Value Percentage	P	826	1-3	826	1-3	826	1-3
Cash Flow	F	002600	1-6	002600	1-6	002600	1-6
Depreciation Percentage	R	200	1-3	167	1-3	143	1-3

		Value	Range	Value	Range	Value	Range
Present Value Percentage	P	751	1-3	751	1-3	751	1-3
Cash Flow	F	002600	1-6	002600	1-6	002600	1-6
Depreciation Percentage	R	200	1-3	167	1-3	143	1-3
Present Value Percentage	P	683	1-3	683	1-3	683	1-3
Cash Flow	F	002600	1-6	002600	1-6	002600	1-6
Depreciation Percentage	R	200	1-3	167	1-3	143	1-3
Present Value Percentage	P	621	1-3	621	1-3	621	1-3
Cash Flow	F			002600	1-6	002600	1-6
Depreciation Percentage	R			167	1-3	143	1-3
Present Value Percentage	P			564	1-3	564	1-3
Cash Flow	F					002600	1-6
Depreciation Percentage	R					143	1-3
Present Value Percentage	P					513	1-3
Probability	E	20	1-2	20	1-2	60	1-2

OUTPUT

	Excess Present Value	Probability	Expected Excess Present Value
5 Years	$(799.01)	.20	$(159.80)
6 Years	(503.78)	.20	(100.76)
7 Years	(44.50)	.60	(26.70)
Total Expected Present Value			$(287.26)

FORTRAN PROGRAM TO DETERMINE
PURCHASE COST
FOR CHAPTER 2 — ILLUSTRATION 8

Program Step		Reference to Flowchart Step and/or Explanation
5	DIMENSION X (100), Y(100), Y(100), Z(100)	
7	FORMAT (1X, 'INPUT PURCHASE COST')	
8	WRITE (6,7)	To Format the Input
9	FORMAT (F7.0)	To Input Purchase Cost
10	READ (5,9)C	
12	FORMAT (1X, 'INPUT NO. OF ESTIMATES')	To Provide User Instructions
14	WRITE (6,12)	To Format the Input
18	FORMAT (12)	To Input Number of Estimates
20	READ (5,18)N	(1)
22	T3 = 0	To Set Grand Total Summing Area
30	DO 255 I = 1,N,1	To Set Loop for Number of Estimates
32	FORMAT (1X, 'INPUT SALVAGE VALUE FOR ESTIMATE', I2)	
34	WRITE (6,32)I	To Provide User Instructions
38	FORMAT (F4.0)	To Format the Input
40	READ (5,38)V	(2) To Input Salvage Value
42	FORMAT (1X, 'INPUT TAX RATE FOR ESTIMATE', I2)	
44	WRITE (6,42)I	To Provide User Instructions
58	FORMAT (F2.2)	To Format the Input
60	READ (5,58)T	(3) To Input Tax Rate

Line	Statement	Comment
62	FORMAT (1X, 'INPUT P.V. % FOR FINAL YEAR')	To Provide User Instructions
64	WRITE (6,62)	To Format the Input
128	FORMAT (F3.3)	
130	READ (5,128)P2	To Input P.V. % for Final Year
139	$D = C - V$	(4) To Compute Depreciable Amount
142	FORMAT (1X, 'INPUT NO. OF YEARS OF LIFE')	To Provide User Instructions
144	WRITE (6,142)	To Format the Input
150	FORMAT (I2)	
151	READ (5,150)L	To Input Number of Years of Life
152	D5 = 0	To Set Up P.V. Summing Area
153	DO 210 J = 1,L,1	To Set Loop for Number of Years of Life
155	FORMAT (1X, 'INPUT DEPREC. % FOR YEAR', I2)	To Provide User Instructions
156	WRITE (6,155)J	To Format the Input
158	FORMAT (F3.3)	
160	READ (5,158)D1	To Input Depreciation %
170	$D2 = D1 * D$	(5) Computations
180	$D3 = D2 * T$	(6) Computations
182	FORMAT (1X, 'INPUT P.V. % FOR YEAR', I2)	To Provide User Instructions
184	WRITE (6,182)J	To Format the Input
188	FORMAT (F3.3)	
190	READ (5,188)P6	To Input P.V. %
200	$D4 = D3*P6$	(7) Computations
210	$D5 = D5 + D4$	(8) Computations
225	$P3 = V*P2$	(9) Computations
230	$P4 = C - (P3 + D5)$	(10) Computations
232	FORMAT (1X, 'INPUT PROBABILITY %')	To Provide User Instructions
234	WRITE (6,232)	To Format the Input
238	FORMAT (F2.2)	

Program Step		Reference to Flowchart Step and/or Explanation
240	READ (5,238)P5	To Input Probability %
250	T2 = P4*P5	(11) To Compute Expected Value of Purchase Cost
252	T3 = T3 + T2	To Sum Up Grand Total
253	X(I) = P4	To Array Output
254	Y(I) = P5	To Array Output
255	Z(I) = T2	To Array Output
256	FORMAT (26X, 'P.V.',26X, 'PROBABILITY',26X, 'EXPECTED P.V.')	To Format the Headings
257	WRITE (6,256)	To Print Headings
258	DO 270 I = 1,N,1	To Set Loop for Printing Output
260	FORMAT (26X, F9.2,21X,F4.2,33X,F9.2)	To Format the Output
270	WRITE (6,260) X (I), Y(I), Z(I)	(12) To Print Output
291	FORMAT (26X, 'TOTAL EXPECTED P.V.', 48X, F9.2)	To Format Grand Total
300	WRITE (6,291)T3	(13) To Print Grand Total
305	STOP	
	END	

EXAMPLE OF INPUT AND OUTPUT FOR FORTRAN COMPUTER PROGRAM TO DETERMINE PURCHASE COST FOR CHAPTER 2 — ILLUSTRATION 8

INPUT

Description of Variable	Variable Name Used in Program	3-Year Life		4-Year Life		5-Year Life		6-Year Life	
		Amount	Columns on Card or Other Type of Input	Amount	Columns on Card Or Other Type of Input	Amount	Columns on Card or Other Type of Input	Amount	Columns on Card or Other Type of Input
Cost	C	0010000	1-7	001500	1-6	001000	1-4	000500	1-6
No. of Estimates	N	04	1-2						
Salvage Value	V	002000	1-6	50	1-2	50	1-2	50	1-2
Tax %	T	50	1-2	683	1-3	621	1-3	564	1-3
P.V. % for Final Yr.	P2	751	1-3	04	1-2	05	1-2	06	1-2
No. of Yrs. of Life	L	03	1-2	250	1-3	200	1-3	166	1-3
Deprec. %	D1	333	1-3	909	1-3	909	1-3	909	1-3
P.V. %	P6	909	1-3	250	1-3	200	1-3	166	1-3
Deprec. %	D1	333	1-3	826	1-3	826	1-3	826	1-3
P.V. %	P6	826	1-3	250	1-3	200	1-3	166	1-3
Deprec. %	D1	333	1-3	751	1-3	751	1-3	751	1-3
P.V. %	P6	751	1-3	250	1-3	200	1-3	166	1-3
Deprec. %	D1								

Description of Variable	Variable Name Used in Program	Amounts	Columns on Card or Other Type of Input	Amount	Columns on Card or Other Type of Input	Amount	Columns on Card or Other Type of Input	Amount	Columns on Card or Other Type of Input
P.V. %	P6			683	1-3	683	1-3	683	1-3
Deprec. %	D1					200		166	1-3
P.V. %	P6					621		621	1-3
Deprec. %	D1							166	1-3
P.V. %	P6							564	1-3
Probability %	P5	10	1-2	40	1-2	40	1-2	10	1-2

OUTPUT

	P.V.	Probability	Expected P.V.
3 Years	$5,186.65	.10	$ 518.67
4 Years	5,608.44	.40	2,243.38
5 Years	5,968.00	.40	2,387.20
6 Years	6,284.87	.10	628.49
Total Expected Value			$5,777.72

FORTRAN PROGRAM TO DETERMINE
LEASE COST
FOR CHAPTER 2 — ILLUSTRATION 11

Program Step		Reference to Flowchart Step and/or Explanation
2	DIMENSION X(100), Y(100), Z(100)	To Provide for Arrays
5	FORMAT (1X, 'INPUT LEASE COST')	
6	WRITE (6,5)	To Provide User Instructions
8	FORMAT (F6.0)	To Format the Input
10	READ (5,8)CL	(1) To Input Lease Cost
12	FORMAT (1X, 'INPUT TAX RATE')	
14	WRITE (6,12)	To Provide User Instructions
18	FORMAT (F2.2)	To Format Input
20	READ (5,18)T	To Input Tax Rate
24	FORMAT ('INPUT NO. OF ESTIMATES')	
26	WRITE (6,24)	To Provide User Instructions
28	FORMAT (12)	To Format Input
30	READ (5,28)N	To Input Number of Estimates
31	T1 = 0	To Set Up Grand Total Summing Area
40	DO 98 I = 1,N,1	To Set Loop for Number of Estimates
42	FORMAT (1X,'INPUT P.V. % FOR ESTIMATE', 12)	
44	WRITE (6,42)I	To Provide User Instructions
58	FORMAT (F4.3)	To Format Input
60	READ (5,58)V	To Input P.V. %
70	V1 = (1 − T) *CL	(2) To Compute Lease Payment Net of Tax
71	P2 = V1 *V	(3) To Compute P.V. of Net Lease Payments

	Program Step	Reference to Flowchart Step and/or Explanation
74	FORMAT (1X, 'INPUT PROBABILITY % FOR ESTIMATE', 12)	To Provide User Instructions
75	WRITE (6,74)I	To Format Input
78	FORMAT (F2.2)	
80	READ (5,78)P	To Input Probability %
90	P1 = P2 * P	(4) To Compute Expected Value Cost of Net Lease Payments
92	X(I) = P2	To Provide Output Arrays
93	Y(I) = P	To Provide Output Arrays
94	Z(I) = P1	To Provide Output Arrays
98	T1 = T1 + P1	(5) To Sum Up Expected Value Costs
100	FORMAT (26X, 'P.V.',26X,'PROBABILITY', 26X,'EXPECTED P.V.')	To Format Headings
101	WRITE (6,100)	To Print Headings
103	DO 110 I = 1,N,I	To Set Loop for Output Printout
105	FORMAT (26X,F9.2,21X,F4.21X,F4.2,33X,F9.2)	To Format Output
110	WRITE (6,105) X (I),Y(I),Z(I)	To Print Totals
140	FORMAT (26X,'TOTAL EXPECTED P.V.',48X,F9.2)	To Format Grand Total
150	WRITE (6,140)T1	To Print Grand Total
160	STOP	
	END	

EXAMPLE OF INPUT AND OUTPUT FOR
FORTRAN COMPUTER PROGRAM TO
DETERMINE LEASE COST
FOR CHAPTER 2 — ILLUSTRATION 11

INPUT

Description of Variable	Variable Name Used in Program	3-Year Life Amount	3-Year Life Columns on Card or Other Type of Input	4-Year Life Amount	4-Year Life Columns on Card or Other Type of Input	5-Year Life Amount	5-Year Life Columns on Card or Other Type of Input	6-Year Life Amount	6-Year Life Columns on Card or Other Type of Input
Cost	CL	003000	1-6						
Tax Rate	T	50	1-2						
No. of Estimates	N	04	1-2						
P.V. %	V	2486	1-4	3169	1-4	3790	1-4	4354	1-4
Probability	P	10	1-2	40	1-2	40	1-2	10	1-2

OUTPUT

	P.V.	Probability	Expected P.V.
3 Years	$3,729.00	.10	$ 372.90
4 Years	4,753.50	.40	1,901.40
5 Years	5,685.00	.40	2,274.00
6 Years	6,531.00	.10	653.10
Total Expected P.V.			$5,201.40

FORTRAN PROGRAM TO DETERMINE CONTROL LIMITS
USING THE STANDARD DEVIATION TECHNIQUE
FOR CHAPTER 3 — ILLUSTRATION 6

Program Step		Reference to Flowchart Step and/or Explanation
5	FORMAT (1X,'INPUT NO. OF SAMPLES')	To Provide User Instructions
6	WRITE (6,5)	
8	FORMAT (12)	To Format Input
10	READ (5,8)N	To Input the Standard Deviation Size
11	S1 = 0	To Set Up Standard Deviation Summing Area
12	T1 = 0	To Set Up Standard Deviation Summing Area
13	SN = N	To Change Variable to Real Mode
20	DO 52 I = 1,N,1	To Set Up Loop for the Number of Samples
22	FORMAT (1X, 'INPUT SAMPLE NO.',12)	To Provide User Instructions
24	WRITE (6,22)I	To Format Input
*28	FORMAT (4F4.2)	(3) To Input Each Sample
*30	READ (5,28)A,B,C,D	(3a)
*40	S = (A + B + C + D)/4	(3a)
50	S1 = S1 + S	(3b)
51	T = S*S	(3b)
52	T1 = T1 + T	(3c)
70	S2 = S1/SN	(3d)
80	S3 = S2*S2	(3d)
90	S4 = S3*SN	(3e)
100	S5 = T1 − S4	(3f)
110	S6 = S5/(SN − 1)	
120	S7 = SQRT (S6)	(3g) To Compute Standard Deviation

```
122    FORMAT (1X, 'INPUT STAN. DEV. MULTIPLE')
124    WRITE (6,122)
128    FORMAT (F3.2)
130    READ (5,128)SM

140    SL = SM*S7
150    SL1 = S2 + SL
160    SL2 = S2 - SL
165    FORMAT (22X,'STANDARD',22X,'UPPER CONTROL
       LIMIT',22X,'LOWER CONTROL LIMIT')
166    WRITE (6,165)
170    FORMAT (22X, F6.2,24X,F6.2,35X,F6.2)
180    WRITE (6,170)S2,SL1,SL2
190    STOP
END
```

	To Provide User Instructions
(4)	To Input Appropriate Multiple of the Standard Deviation Associated with the Desired Reliability
(5)	To Compute Amount Used for Control Limits
(5a)	To Compute Upper Control Limit
(5b)	To Compute Lower Control Limit
	To Set Up Headings
	To Print Headings
	To Format Output
	To Print Amounts

*If a larger sample size is needed, change these steps, e.g., if 8 is used

```
FORMAT (8F4.2)
READ (5,28)A,B,C,D,E,F,G,H
S = (A + B + C + D + E + F + G + H)/8
```

EXAMPLE OF INPUT AND OUTPUT FOR FORTRAN COMPUTER PROGRAM TO DETERMINE STATISTICAL CONTROL LIMITS FOR CHAPTER 3 — ILLUSTRATION 6

INPUT

Description of Variable	Variable Name Used in Program	Amounts A	B	C	D	Columns on Card or Other Type of Input
Sample Size	SN	09				1-2
Samples	A,B,C,D	1880	2200	2100	2400	1-16
Samples	A,B,C,D	1900	1900	2100	2300	1-16
Samples	A,B,C,D	2400	2300	2200	2460	1-16
Samples	A,B,C,D	1950	2360	2200	2190	1-16
Samples	A,B,C,D	2500	2210	2250	2480	1-16
Samples	A,B,C,D	2670	2250	2450	2430	1-16
Samples	A,B,C,D	2860	2500	2600	2680	1-16
Samples	A,B,C,D	1950	2420	2220	2610	1-16
Samples	A,B,C,D	2550	2000	2350	2780	1-16
Standard Deviation Multiple	SM	164				1-3

OUTPUT

Standard	Upper Control Limit	Lower Control Limit
23.24	26.33	20.16

FORTRAN PROGRAM TO DETERMINE
REGRESSION LINE AND COEFFICIENT OF DETERMINATION
RELATIONSHIP WITH ACTIVITY
FOR CHAPTER 4 — ILLUSTRATIONS 10 AND 11

	Program Step	Reference to Flowchart Step	and/or Explanation
2	DIMENSION A(100),R(100),EK(100)		To Set Up Array for Output
5	FORMAT (1X,'INPUT NO. OF PERIODS')		
6	WRITE (6,5)		
8	FORMAT (I2)		To Format Input
10	READ (5,8)N	(2)	To Input Number of Periods
11	T1 = 0		To Set Up Summing Area for Activity Level Amount
12	T2 = 0		To Set Up Summing Area for Cost
13	T3 = 0		To Set Up Summing Area for Activity Level Squared Amount
14	T4 = 0		To Set Up Summing Area for Hours Times Cost Squared
16	T = 0		To Set Up Summing Area for Actual Costs
20	DO 100 I = 1,N,1		To Set Loop for Number of Periods
22	FORMAT (1X,'INPUT ACTIV. LEVEL AND COST FOR PERIOD',I2)		
24	WRITE (6,22)I		
28	FORMAT (2F6.0)		To Format Input
30	READ (5,28)UK,E	(2a)	To Input Activity Level and Cost
35	A(I) = UK		To Array Activity Level Amounts
40	T1 = T1 + UK	(2a)	To Sum Up Activity Level Amounts
45	T = T + E		To Sum Up Actual Costs
55	PN = N		To Change Variable to Real Mode
60	T2 = T2 + E	(2a)	To Sum Up Cost

Program Step		Reference to Flowchart Step and/or Explanation
70	UK1 = UK*UK	(3) To Square Activity Level Amounts
80	T3 = T3 + UK1	(3) To Sum Up Squared Hours Amounts
90	E1 = UK*E	(3a) To Multiply Activity Level Amounts Times Cost
100	T4 = T4 + E1	(3a) To Sum Up Previous Products
120	T5 = T2*(T1/PN)	(4) To Multiply Total Cost Times Total Activity Level Amounts Divided by Number of Periods
130	T6 = T1*(T1/PN)	(4a) To Compute Average Activity Level Amount
140	T7 = T4 – T5	(3) To Subtract (4) Total from (3a) Total
150	T8 = T3 – T6	(5a) To Subtract (4a) Total from (3) Total
160	T9 = T7/T8	(6) To Divide (5) Total by (5a) Total and Derive Variable Cost
170	F = T9*T1	(7) To Multiply (6) Total Times Activity Level Amount
180	F1 = T2 – F	(7a) To Subtract (7) Total from Total Cost
190	F2 = F1/PN	(7b) To Divide (7a) Total by Number of Periods and Derive Fixed Cost
195	FORMAT (26X,'FIXED COST',36X,'VARIABLE COST')	To Set Up Headings for Fixed and Variable Costs
196	WRITE (6,195)	To Print Headings
200	FORMAT (36X,F10.2,36X,F10.8)	To Format Output for Fixed and Variable Cost
210	WRITE (6,200)F2,T9	To Print Fixed and Variable Cost
211	FORMAT (/67X,'REGRESSION LINE')	To Set Up Headings for Regression Line
212	WRITE (6,211)	To Print Headings
220	DO 240 I = 1,N;1	To Set Up Loop for Regression Line Calculations
240	R(I) = F2 +(9*A(I))	To Obtain Regression Line
245	DO 260 I = 1,N,1	To Set Up Loop for Regression Line Printout
250	FORMAT (59X, F10.2)	To Format Output for Regression Line
260	WRITE (6,250)R(I)	To Print Regression Line
270	S1 = 0	To Set Up Summing Area

```
280    S3 = 0                                                    To Set Up Summing Area
290    DO 360 I = 1,N,1
300    A1 = T/PN
310    D = EK(I) - R(I)
320    S = D*D
330    S1 = S1 + S
340    D1 = EK(I) - A1
350    S2 = D1*D1
360    S3 = S3 + S2
370    S4 = S1/(PN - 2)
380    S5 = S3/(PN - 2)
390    C = S4/S5
400    C1 = 1 - C
405    FORMAT (/52X, 'COEFFICIENT OF DETERMINATION')           To Format Output
407    WRITE (6,405)                                             To Print Data
410    FORMAT (63X,F10.4)
420    WRITE (6,410)C1
430    STOP
END
```

EXAMPLE OF INPUT AND OUTPUT FOR
FORTRAN COMPUTER PROGRAM TO DETERMINE
REGRESSION LINE AND COEFFICIENT OF DETERMINATION
FOR CHAPTER 4 — ILLUSTRATIONS 10 AND 11

INPUT

Description of Variable	Variable Name Used in Program	Amounts		Columns on Card or Other Type of Input
		Activity Level	Cost	
No. of Periods	N	10		1-2
Activity Level and Cost	uk,E	010019	000078	1-12
Activity Level and Cost	uk,E	011904	000094	1-12
Activity Level and Cost	uk,E	013638	000110	1-12
Activity Level and Cost	uk,E	015622	000127	1-12
Activity Level and Cost	uk,E	019431	000151	1-12
Activity Level and Cost	uk,E	022774	000175	1-12
Activity Level and Cost	uk,E	026058	000183	1-12
Activity Level and Cost	uk,E	031354	000210	1-12
Activity Level and Cost	uk,E	035900	000255	1-12
Activity Level and Cost	uk,E	041895	000317	1-12

OUTPUT

Fixed Cost	Variable Cost
12.40	.00689424

Regression Line

81.47
94.47
106.42
120.10
146.36
169.41
192.05
228.56
259.90
301.24

Coefficient of Determination

.9835

PROGRAM TO DETERMINE REGRESSION LINE—RELATIONSHIP WITH TIME FOR CHAPTER 4 — ILLUSTRATION 12

	Program Step	Flowchart Step	Reference to Flowchart Step and/or Explanation
2	DIMENSION R(100),PX(100)		To Array Variables
5	FORMAT (1X,'INPUT NO. OF PERIODS')		To Provide User Instructions
6	WRITE (6,5)		To Format Input
8	FORMAT (12)		
10	READ (5,8)N	(1)	To Input Number of Periods
11	P1 = 0		To Set Up Summing Area
12	S1 = 0		To Set Up Summing Area
13	T1 = 0		To Set Up Summing Area
14	T3 = 0		To Set Up Summing Area
20	DO 100 I = 1,N,1		To Set Loop for Number of Periods
22	FORMAT (1X,'INPUT PERIOD NO. AND AMOUNT FOR PERIOD,'12)		To Format Input
24	WRITE (6,22)I		To Input User Instructions
28	FORMAT (F2.0, F6.0)		To Format Input
30	READ (5,28)P,S	(1a)	To Input Period and Amount
32	PX (II) = P		To Array Periods
40	P1 = P1 + P	(1a)	To Sum Up Periods
60	S1 = S1 + S	(1a)	To Sum Up Amounts
70	T = P*P	(2)	Computations
80	T1 = T1 + T	(2a)	Computations
90	T2 = S*P	(2a)	Computations
100	T3 = T3 + T2	(2a)	Computations

```
115   PN = N                                          To Change Variable to Floating Point Mode
120   PM = P1/PN                                      (2b) Computations
130   PM1 = S1/PN                                     (2c) Computations
140   B = T3 – (PM *S1)                               (3)  Computations
150   B1 = T1 – (PM *P1)                              (3a) Computations
160   B2 = B/B1                                       (3b) Computations
170   A = B2*PM                                       (3c) Computations
180   A1 = PM1 – A                                    (3d) Computations
184   FORMAT (35X,'FIXED AMOUNT',35X,
          'VARIABLE AMOUNT')
186   WRITE (6,184)                                   To Provide User Instructions
190   FORMAT (35X,F10.2,37X,F10.2)                    To Format Output
200   WRITE (6,190)A1, B2                             To Print Output
210   DO 220 I = 1,N,1                                To Set Loop for Calculation of Regression Line Amounts
220   R(I) = A1 + (PX(I) *B2)                         To Calculate Regression Line Amounts
225   FORMAT (59X, 'REGRESSION LINE')                 To Set Up Headings
230   WRITE (6,225)                                   To Print Headings
238   DO 245 I = 1,N,1                                To Set Loop for Output of Data
240   FORMAT (59X,F10.2)                              To Format Output
245   WRITE (6,240) R (I)                             To Print Output
250   STOP
      END
```

**EXAMPLE OF INPUT AND OUTPUT FOR
FORTRAN COMPUTER PROGRAM TO DETERMINE
REGRESSION LINE—RELATIONSHIP WITH TIME
FOR CHAPTER 4 — ILLUSTRATION 12**

INPUT

Description of Variable	Variable Name Used in Program	Amounts		Columns on Card or Other Type of Input
		Period	Amount	
No. of Periods	N	10		1-2
Period and Amount	P,S	00	010019	1-8
Period and Amount	P,S	01	011904	1-8
Period and Amount	P,S	02	013638	1-8
Period and Amount	P,S	03	015622	1-8
Period and Amount	P,S	04	019431	1-8
Period and Amount	P,S	05	022774	1-8
Period and Amount	P,S	06	026058	1-8

Period and Amount	P,S	07	031354	1-8
Period and Amount	P,S	08	035900	1-8
Period and Amount	P,S	09	041895	1-8

OUTPUT

Fixed Amount	Variable Amount
7093.49	3503.56

Regression Line

7093.49
10597.05
14100.61
17604.16
21107.72
24611.28
28114.84
31618.39
35121.35
38625.51

179

PROGRAM TO DETERMINE THE AMOUNTS IN THE EXPONENTIAL SMOOTHING TECHNIQUE FOR CHAPTER 5 — ILLUSTRATION 6

	Program Step	Reference to Flowchart Step and/or Explanation
2	DIMENSION PER (100), AC(100), ES(100)	To Provide for Arrays
5	FORMAT (1X, 'INPUT INITIAL ACTUAL SALES AMOUNT')	
6	WRITE (6,5)	To Provide User Instructions
18	FORMAT (F6.0)	To Format Input
20	READ (5,18)S1	(1) To Input Initial Actual Sales Amount
22	FORMAT (1X, 'INPUT INITIAL SALES ESTIMATE')	
24	WRITE (6,22)	To Provide User Instructions
30	READ (5,18)E1	(2) To Input Initial Sales Estimate
46	NF = 01	To Input Period 1
52	FORMAT (1X, 'INPUT NO. OF PERIODS')	
54	WRITE (6,52)	To Provide User Information
56	FORMAT (I2)	To Format Input
58	READ (5,56)N	To Input Number of Periods
60	FORMAT (1X, 'INPUT ALPHA CONSTANT')	
62	WRITE (6,60)	To Provide User Instructions
64	FORMAT (F2.2)	To Format Input
66	READ (5,64)A	To Input Alpha Constant
70	DO 160 I = 1,N,1	To Set Loop for Rest of Periods
72	FORMAT (1X, 'INPUT ACTUAL SALES FOR PERIODS', I2)	

Line	Code		Comment
74	WRITE (6,72)I		To Provide User Instructions
78	FORMAT (F6.0)		To Format Input
80	READ (5,78)S		To Input Actual Sales for Previous Period
82	K = I + 1		To Add 1 to Counter
84	FORMAT (1X, 'INPUT PERIOD NO. AND ACTUAL SALES FOR PERIOD', I2)		
86	WRITE (6,84)K		To Provide User Instructions
88	FORMAT (I2,F6.0)		To Format Input
90	READ (5,88)NP,S3		To Input Period Number and Actual Sales for Current Period
110	S2 = S * A	(3)	Computations
120	E2 = E1*(1 − A)	(3a)	Computations
130	E3 = S2 + E2	(3b)	Computations
145	E1 = E3		To Move Previous Sales Estimate to Next Loop
150	PER (I) = NP		To Array Output
155	AC(I) = S3		To Array Output
160	ES(I) = E3		To Array Output
170	FORMAT (24X, 'PERIOD',24X,'ACTUAL AMOUNT', 24X, 'ESTIMATED AMOUNT')		
180	WRITE (6,170)		To Set Up Headings
190	FORMAT (26X,F4.0,28X,F8.0,30X,F8.0)		To Print Headings
200	WRITE (6,190)FN,S1,E1		To Format Output
205	DO 210 I = 1,N,1		To Output First Line of Output
210	WRITE (6,190)PER(I),AC(I),ES(I)		To Output Rest of Output
220	STOP		
	END		

EXAMPLE OF INPUT AND OUTPUT FOR FORTRAN COMPUTER PROGRAM TO DETERMINE THE AMOUNTS IN THE EXPONENTIAL SMOOTHING TECHNIQUE FOR CHAPTER 5 — ILLUSTRATION 6

INPUT

Description of Variable	Variable Name Used in Program	Amounts	Columns on Card or Other Type of Input
Initial Actual Sales	S1	010019	1-6
Initial Estimate of Sales	E1	009800	1-6
No. of Periods	N	10	1-2
Alpha Constant	A	20	1-2
Actual Sales for Previous Period	S	010019	1-6
Period No. and Actual Sales for Current Period	NP,S3	02 011904	1-8
Prev. Period	S	011904	1-6
Curr. Period	NP,S3	03 011000	1-8
Prev. Period	S	011000	1-6

Curr. Period	NP,S3	04	010055	1-8
Prev. Period	S	010055		1-6
Curr. Period	NP,S3	05	014212	1-8
Prev. Period	S	014212		1-6
Curr. Period	NP,S3	06	016015	1-8
Prev. Period	S	016015		1-6
Curr. Period	NP,S3	07	012904	1-8
Prev. Period	S	012904		1-6
Curr. Period	NP,S3	08	014000	1-8
Prev. Period	S	014000		1-6
Curr. Period	NP,S3	09	015200	1-8
Prev. Period	S	015200		1-6
Curr. Period	NP,S3	10	015100	1-8
Prev. Period	S	015100		1-6
Curr. Period	NP,S3	11	000000	1-8

OUTPUT

Period	Actual Amount	Estimated Amount
1	$10,019	$ 9,800
2	11,904	9,844
3	11,000	10,256
4	10,055	10,405
5	14,212	10,335
6	16,015	11,110
7	12,904	12,091
8	14,000	12,254
9	15,200	12,603
10	15,100	13,122
11	—	13,518

PROGRAM TO DEMONSTRATE STEPS IN ALLOCATING ADVERTISING DOLLARS TO SEGMENTS FOR CHAPTER 6 — ILLUSTRATION 9

Program Step	Reference to Flowchart Step and/or Explanation
2 DIMENSION ST1(100),ST2(100),ST3(100), ST4(100)	To Provide Arrays
4 X = 0	
5 FORMAT (1X, 'INPUT NO. OF SEGMENTS')	To Provide User Instructions
6 WRITE (6,5)	To Format Input
8 FORMAT (I2)	To Input the Number of Territories
10 READ (5,8)N	To Set Loop for Number of Territories
20 NU = 0	To Test Loop for Number of Territories
21 IF (N − NU) 126,126,23	
22 FORMAT (1X, 'INPUT SEGMENT NO.')	To Provide User Instructions
23 WRITE (6,22)	To Input Territory Number
25 READ 8,NT	
26 FORMAT (1X, 'INPUT CONT. MARGIN % AND SALES FOR SEGMENT', I2)	To Provide User Instructions
27 WRITE (6,26)NT	To Format Input
28 FORMAT (F2.2,F6.2)	(1) (1a) To Input Contribution Margin and Sales for % Each Segment
30 READ (5,28)P,S	(1b)
50 CM = P*S	
60 IF (NT − 2) 62,90,62	To Branch to Step 90
62 IF (NT − 3) 70,110,70	To Branch to Step 110
70 CM1 = CM	To Store Territory 1 Margin

Line	Code	Comment
78	NU = NU + 1	
80	GO TO 21	To Branch to Step 21
90	CM2 = CM	To Store Territory 2 Margin
98	NU = NU + 1	
100	GO TO 21	To Branch to Step 21
110	CM3 = CM	To Store Territory 3 Margin
118	NU = NU + 1	
120	GO TO 21	
124	FORMAT (1X, 'INPUT THE TOTAL MAXIMUM')	To Format Input (2)
126	WRITE (6,124)	
128	FORMAT (F6.0)	
130	READ (5,128)A	
134	FORMAT (1X, 'INPUT MAXIMUM FOR ALL THREE SEGMENTS')	
136	WRITE (6,134)	
155	FORMAT (3F6.0)	To Format Input (3)
160	READ (5,155)A1,A2,A3	Adv. Maximum for the Territories
164	FORMAT (1X, 'INPUT THE NO. OF FEASIBLE OPTIONS')	
166	WRITE (6,164)	To Input Number of Feasible Solutions
170	READ (5,8) K	To Set Loop for Number of Feasible Solutions
180	DO 994 J = 1,K,1	
184	FORMAT (1X, 'INPUT THE NO.',I2)	To Input Feasible Options
186	WRITE (6,184)J	
190	READ (5,8)M	
200	IF (M − 2) 210,380,210	To Choose Option Number 2
210	IF (M − 3) 220,510,220	To Choose Option Number 3
220	IF (M − 4) 230,640,230	To Choose Option Number 4

	Program Step	Reference to Flowchart Step and/or Explanation
230	IF (M − 5) 240,770,240	To Choose Option Number 5
240	IF (M − 6) 250,900,250	To Choose Option Number 6
250	C1 = A1*CM1	(5a)
260	IF ((A − A1) − A2) 290,270,270	To Test Territory 2 Maximum
270	C2 = A2*CM2	(5a)
280	GO TO 300	
290	C2 = (A − A1)*CM2	(5a)
300	IF ((A − (A1 + A2)) − A3) 330,310,310	To Test Territory 3 Maximum
310	C3 = A3*CM3	(5a)
320	GO TO 340	
330	C3 = (A − (A1 + A2)) * CM3	(5a)
332	IF (C1)333,334,334	
333	C1 = 0	
334	IF (C2)335,336,336	
335	C2 = 0	
336	IF (C3)337,340,340	
337	C3 = 0	
340	C4 = C1 + C2 + C3	To Obtain Total Territory Margin
370	GO TO 990	
380	C1 = A1*CM1	(5a)
390	IF ((A − A1) − A3) 420, 400, 400	To Test Territory 3 Maximum
400	C3 = A3*CM3	(5a)
410	GO TO 430	
420	C3 = (A − A1)*CM3	(5a)
430	IF ((A − (A1 + A3)) − A2)460,440,440	To Test Territory 2 Maximum
440	C2 = A2*CM2	(5a)

```
450   GO TO 470
460   C2 = (A − (A1 +A3) ) *CM2                          (5a)
462   IF(C1)463,464,464
463   C1 = 0
464   IF (C2) 465,466,466
465   C2 = 0
466   IF (C3)467,470,470
467   C3 = 0
470   C4 = C1 + C2 C3                                     To Obtain Total Territory Margin
500   GO TO 990
510   C2 = A2 *CM2                                        (5a)  To Test Territory 1 Maximum
520   IF ( (A − A2) − A1) 550,530,530                     (5a)
530   C1 = A1 *CM1
540   GO TO 560
550   C1 = (A − A2) *CM1                                  (5a)  To Test Territory 3 Maximum
560   IF ( (A − (A2 + A1) − A3) 590,570,570               (5a)
570   C3 = A3 'CM3
580   GO TO 600
590   C3 = (A − (A2 + A1) ) *CM3                          (5a)
592   IF (C1) 593,594,594
593   C1 = 0
594   IF (C2)595,596,596
595   C2 = 0
596   IF (C3)597,600,600
597   C3 = 0
600   C4 = C1 + C2 + C3                                   To Obtain Total Territory Margin
630   GO TO 990
640   C2 = A2 *CM2                                        (5a)  To Test Territory 3 Maximum
650   IF ( (A − A2) − A3) 680,660,660
```

Program Step	Reference to Flowchart Step and/or Explanation
660 C3 = A3*CM3	(5a)
670 GO TO 690	(5a)
680 C3 = (A − A2)*CM3	To Test Territory 1 Maximum
690 IF ((A − (A2 + A3)) − A1) 720,700,700	(5a)
700 C1 = A1*CM1	(5a)
710 GO TO 730	
720 C1 = (A − (A2 + A3))*CM1	
722 IF (C1) 723,724,724	
723 C1 = 0	
724 IF (C2)725,726,726	
725 C2 = 0	
726 IF (C3) 727,730,730	
727 C3 = 0	
730 C4 = C1 + C2 + C3	To Obtain Total Territory Margin
760 GO TO 990	(5a)
770 C3 = A3*CM3	To Test Territory 1 Maximum
780 IF ((A − A3) − A1) 810,790,790	(5a)
790 C1 = A1*CM1	
800 GO TO 820	(5a)
810 C1 = (A − A3) * CM1	
820 IF ((A − (A1 + A3)) − A2) 850,830,830	To Test Territory 2 Maximum
830 C2 = A2*CM2	
840 GO TO 860	(5a)
850 C2 = (A − (A1 + A3))*CM2	(5a)
852 IF (C1) 853,854,854	
853 C1 = 0	
854 IF (C2) 855,856,856	

```
855   C2 = 0
856   IF (C3) 857,860,860
857   C3 = 0
860   C4 = C1 + C2 + C3                          To Obtain Total Territory Margin
890   GO TO 990
900   C3 = A3*CM3                          (5a)
910   IF ( (A – A3) – A2) 920,912,912      (5a)  To Test Territory 2 Maximum
912   C2 = A2*CM2
915   GO TO 925
920   C2 = (A – A3)*CM2                    (5a)
925   IF ( (A – (A3 +A2) ) – A1) 940,930,930   (5a)  To Test Territory 1 Margin
930   C1 = A1*CM1
935   GO TO 950
940   C1 = (A – (A3 + A2) )*CM1            (5a)
942   IF (C1) 943,944,944
943   C1 = 0
944   IF (C2) 945,946,946
945   C2 = 0
946   IF (C3) 947,950,950
947   C3 = 0
950   C4 = C1 + C2 + C3                          To Obtain Total Territory Margin
970   IF (X) 990,980,990
975   FORMAT (21X, 'TERR. 1', 21X, 'TERR. 2',
      21X, 'TERR. 3', 21X, 'TOTAL')
980   WRITE (6,975)                              To Format Headings
985   X = X +1                                   To Output Headings
990   ST1(J) = C1                                To Array Output
991   ST2(J) = C2                                To Array Output
992   ST3(J) = C3                                To Array Output
```

189

Program Step	Reference to Flowchart Step and/or Explanantion
994 ST4(J) = C4	To Array Output
995 DO 997 J= 1,K,1	To Set Loop for Printout of Output
996 FORMAT (21X,F7.0,21X,F7.0,21X,F7.0, 21X,F7.0)	To Format Output
997 WRITE (6,996)ST1(J),ST2(J),ST3(J),ST4(J)	To Print Output
998 STOP	
END	

**EXAMPLE OF INPUT AND OUTPUT FOR
COMPUTER PROGRAM TO DETERMINE STEPS
IN ALLOCATING DOLLARS TO SEGMENTS
FOR CHAPTER 6 — ILLUSTRATION 9**

INPUT

Description of Variable Used in Program	Variable Name Used in Program	Amounts	Card Columns or Other Input Device Used
No. of Segments	N	03	1-2
Segment No.	NT	01	1-2
Contribution Margin % Sales	P,S	40	
Dollars		000300	1-8
Segment No.	NT	02	1-2
Contribution Margin % Sales	P,S	30	
Dollars		000350	1-8
Segment No.	NT	03	1-2
Contribution Margin % Sales	P,S	40	
Dollars		000350	1-8

Description of Variable Used in Program	Variable Name Used in Program	Amounts			Card Columns or Other Input Device Used
Total Maximum for All Program	A	020000			1-6
Maximum for All Segments	A1, A2, A3	010000	015000	008000	1-18
No. of Feasible Options	K	06			1-2
Option 1	M	01			1-2
Option 2	M	02			1-2
Option 3	M	03			1-2
Option 4	M	04			1-2
Option 5	M	05			1-2
Option 6	M	06			1-2

OUTPUT

	Terr. 1	Terr. 2	Terr. 3	Total
1,2,3	$12,000	$10,500	$ -0-	$22,500
1,3,2	12,000	2,100	11,200	25,300
2,1,3	6,000	15,750	-0-	21,750
2,3,1	-0-	15,750	7,000	22,750
3,1,2	12,000	2,100	11,200	25,300
3,2,1	-0-	12,600	11,200	23,800

FORTRAN PROGRAM TO DETERMINE PRECISION
FOR VARIABLE SAMPLING APPLICATION
FOR CHAPTER 8

Program Step		Reference to Flowchart Step and/or Explanation
5	Z = 0	To Set Up Counter
10	T1 = 0	To Set Up Counter
15	T2 = 0	To Set Up Counter
20	T3 = 0	To Set Up Counter
25	T4 = 0	To Set Up Counter
30	T5 = 0	To Set Up Counter
35	T6 = 0	To Set Up Counter
36	FORMAT (1X, 'INPUT SAMPLE SIZE USED IN ATTRIBUTE TEST FOLLOWED BY BOOK AND AUDIT AMOUNT OF EACH SAMPLE')	
37	WRITE (6,36)	To Format Input
38	FORMAT (I3)	To Input the Sample Size
40	READ (5,38)N	
45	SN = N	To Change Variable to Floating Point
50	DO 105 I = 1, N,1	To Set Loop for the Input of Samples
53	FORMAT (2F7.2)	To Format Input
55	READ (5,53)B,C	(4) Computations
60	D = C − B	(4a) Computations
65	B1 = B*B	(4b) Computations
70	D1 = D*D	(4c) Computations
75	B2 = B*D	(4d) Computations
80	T1 = T1 + B	(4e) Computations

	Program Step	Reference to Flowchart Step and/or Explanation
85	T2 = T2 + C	(4f) Computations
90	T3 = T3 + D	(4g) Computations
95	T4 = T4 + B1	(4h) Computations
100	T5 = T5 + D1	(4i) Computations
105	T6 = T6 + B2	(4j) Computations
115	S1 = T3/T1	(5) Computations
120	S2 = S1*S1	(5a) Computations
125	S3 = S1 + S1	(5b) Computations
130	S4 = T4*S2	(5c) Computations
135	S5 = S3*T6	(5d) Computations
140	S6 = T5 + S4	(5e) Computations
145	S7 = S6 – S5	(5f) Computations
150	S8 = S7/(SN – 1)	(5g) Computations
155	S9 = SQRT(S8)	(5h) Computations
160	FORMAT (1X, 'INPUT RELIABILITY FACTOR AND NO. OF POPULATION ELEMENTS')	
165	WRITE (6,160)	To Format the Input
168	FORMAT (F3.2,F5.0)	To Input the Reliability Factor and the
170	READ (5,168)R,P	Number of Elements in the Population
175	P1 = S9*R*P	(6) To Calculate Precision
180	P3 = P1/SQRT (SN)	(6a) To Calculate Precision
185	P2 = P3*SQRT (1 – (SN/P))	(6b) To Calculate Precision
190	FORMAT (1X, 'INPUT THE POPULATION BOOK VALUE')	
195	WRITE (6,190)	

```
198    FORMAT (F8.2)                              To Format Input
200    READ (5,198)T7                             To Input the Population Book Amount
205    T8 = T7*(1 + S1)                      (7)  To Calculate the Population Estimate
210    R1 = T8 + P2                          (8)  To Calculate Upper Precision Range
215    R2 = T8 – P2                          (8a) To Calculate Lower Precision Range
217    FORMAT (47X, 'PRECISION RESULTS ON
       VARIABLE SAMPLING')
218    WRITE (6,127)                              To Format Output
220    FORMAT (51X, 'THE ESTIMATED TOTAL IS',     To Print Estimate of Population Total
       2X, F10.2)
225    WRITE (6,220)T8
230    FORMAT (43X, 'THE PRECISION RANGE IS', 2X, To Print the Precision Range Around the
       F10.2, 2X, F10.2)                             Population Estimate
240    STOP
       END
```

EXAMPLE OF INPUT AND OUTPUT FOR COMPUTER PROGRAM TO DETERMINE PRECISION FOR VARIABLE SAMPLING APPLICATION FOR CHAPTER 8

INPUT

Description of Variable Used in Program	Variable Name Used in Program	Amounts		Columns for Card or Other Input Device Used
Sample Size	N	030		1-3
Samples, Book Value and Audit Values	B,C	0023000	0024000	1-14
"	B,C	0038000	0038000	1-14
"	B,C	0025000	0025000	1-14
"	B,C	0020000	0021000	1-14
"	B,C	0019500	0019000	1-14
"	B,C	0022500	0022500	1-14
"	B,C	0024200	0024200	1-14
"	B,C	0027300	0027600	1-14
"	B,C	0025000	0023500	1-14
"	B,C	0019500	0019500	1-14
"	B,C	0020200	0020200	1-14
"	B,C	0021600	0021000	1-14
"	B,C	0028100	0028100	1-14
"	B,C	0027100	0027500	1-14

"	B,C	0024000	0023500	1-14
"	B,C	0024100	0023100	1-14
"	B,C	0028100	0028100	1-14
"	B,C	0020200	0020200	1-14
"	B,C	0021200	0021200	1-14
"	B,C	0021500	0021500	1-14
"	B,C	0024400	0024400	1-14
"	B,C	0025800	0024100	1-14
"	B,C	0025500	0025500	1-14
"	B,C	0028100	0028100	1-14
"	B,C	0027500	0027500	1-14
"	B,C	0026000	0026000	1-14
"	B,C	0023000	0023000	1-14
"	B,C	0019800	0019800	1-14
"	B,C	0028900	0028900	1-14
"	B,C	0024900	0024900	1-14
Reliability Factor, No. Elements in Population	R,P	196	00300	1-8
Population Book Value	T7	0735	0000	1-8

OUTPUT

Precision Results on Variable Sampling
The Estimated Total Is 73190.
The Precision Range Is 73755— 72625.

Index

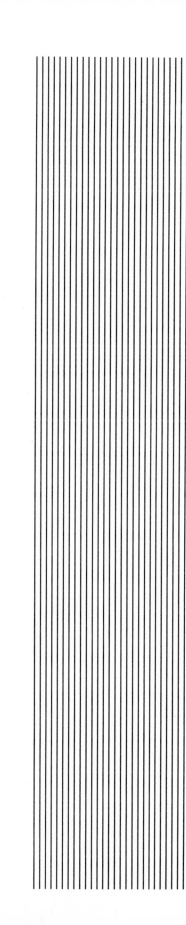